ENDORSEMENTS

If you want to kill giants, you need to hang around giant killers. Leif Hetland is just that—one not intimidated by the impossibilities he faces. *Giant Slayers* gives us the opportunity to come under the influence of one who has truly killed his share of giants—the impossibilities that others run from. While Leif is one of the most courageous individuals I've ever met, he also packs these pages with the wisdom needed to fight the right battles. He is an inspiration to countless numbers of believers worldwide, of which I am one. His obedience and dependence on God have enabled him to see a supernatural invasion of God's power into the most unusual circumstances in life. This book will no doubt impart faith and vision for your own journey into the impossible. At the end of each chapter is a faith-filled declaration. If all you do is agree with and declare those over your life, I'm confident you will be unstoppable in your adventure with God!

BILL JOHNSON
Bethel Church, Redding, CA
Author of *God is Good*

I knew that Leif Hetland was a gifted speaker, but I was not prepared for what an able writer he is. This wonderful, well-written and practical book will help you to overcome obstacles that Satan would put in your way. I warmly recommend this book. After you read it you will want extra copies to give away. A book like this does not come around every day.

R T KENDALL
Minister, Westminster Chapel, London (1977-2002)

Countless people are longing to step into their destiny, and Leif Hetland's new book, *Giant Slayers*, is a Holy Spirit guidebook to overcoming the obstacles that are in your way. If you long to know how to battle the barriers that are keeping you from realizing your purpose in life, this book is for you. I highly recommend it!

KRIS VALLOTTON
Senior Associate Leader, Bethel Church, Redding, CA
CoFounder of Bethel School of Supernatural Ministry
Author of eleven books, including
The Supernatural Ways of Royalty and *Spirit Wars*.

Leif Hetland is a friend and a passionate lover of Jesus as well as a gifted teacher. He has written a powerful guidebook for each of us to be brave and fight the giants before us. He reminds us that before Goliath, David faithfully protected sheep and literally risked his life while no one was watching. You are strong and you are called, in God you have the victory. Whether you are in a lonely field being trained or standing before kings I pray you will take up the weapons God has put in your hands and fight for the Kingdom to advance.

HEIDI G. BAKER, PHD
CoFounder and CEO of Iris Global

Fear aborts your destiny. When you learn how to slay *every* giant in your life, you can step into your unique calling. This book tells you how to get your full reward!

SID ROTH
Host, *It's Supernatural!*

One of the greatest blessings in my life is to be a spiritual son to Leif Hetland. I am one of the many individuals who have been tremendously blessed and transformed by his life and ministry. I am amazed at the favor of God upon him and the love of the Father that he so freely and lavishly imparts to all.

Giant Slayers is Spirit-breathed. It contains valuable insights and revelations we all need to face and defeat our 'giants' as we go in and possess our Promised Land—the fullness of God's destiny and purpose for us. All the inspiring stories of courage, faith, and radical love in this book are nothing short of fleshed out Kingdom principles and revelations demonstrated in our time. This book is both supernatural in inspiration and so practical in application. Drawing out from a deep well of wisdom from decades of serving the Lord faithfully and seeing Him shift atmospheres, heal broken bodies, open closed doors, transform nations, and release Heaven to Earth, the author shares the essential keys to victorious lifestyle. I highly recommend this book to individuals, leaders, churches and movements who are hungry to see the invasion of heaven in every facet of life.

PAUL YADAO

Senior Pastor, Destiny Ministries International, Philippines

We live in particularly uncertain times. The world is now a global village. The economic whirlwinds, threats of violence and war, the tragedy of human displacement and the political vagaries in electoral outcomes anywhere in the world can move us all into challenges we never imagined.

Leif's ministry for decades has been surrounded by all the above as he has ministered the love of God into innumerable people groups in countless countries. Leif's life story is one of overcoming incredible odds. His view from both the valleys of despair and the mountaintops of God's deliverance deeply qualify him to pour out his wisdom on being "a giant slayer".

You will be enriched, challenged, and given wisdom to change as you laugh and cry your way through the powerful insights Leif brings to life on the pages of *Giant Slayers*—ground rules for overcoming life's greatest obstacles.

PETER McHUGH

Senior Minister, Stairway Church, Melbourne, Australia

I loved this book. It was encouraging, inspiring, biblical, and incredibly practical. Life is made up of many obstacles, not just one. This book will help you overcome them. I believe in Leif and commend him and his book to you.

BOB ROBERTS

Senior Pastor, Northwood Church & Author, Keller TX

It has been said that in ministry, who you are counts more than what you say. This is true in the lines of Leif Hetland's wonderful book, *Giant Slayers*. Leif is truly a giant slayer, and he possesses the greatest weapon of Jesus' kingdom more than just about anyone I know...that is the love of God. Drink deeply from the heart of this man when you read his book. You will experience the Father's love, and you will slay your giants, because love casts out fear, and love never fails!

BEN FERRELL
CEO, BMCFerrell, USA

Throughout our lives we are faced with a variety of challenges. It is in these moments that the wisdom of others who have walked the same dark valleys but have overcome prove to be invaluable and sometimes the catalyst for our own personal triumphs and victories. We will all face giants at one time or another and what is so encouraging about Leif Hetland in his book, *Giant Slayers*, is that he is giving us the weapons to defeat any obstacle that would stand in our way thus enabling us to see all that God predestined for us to achieve become a reality.

Your faith and courage will be stirred as you read the pages of this book and because of the authenticity of the author, you will find yourself experiencing the same overcoming power of God in your life. You are called to live a life of greatness so don't allow the giants to intimidate you! Let Leif inspire you to greatness!

RUSSELL AND SAM EVANS
Senior Pastors, Planetshakers

Everyone faces obstacles, but that is not the real problem. The key is our immediate response—a response which makes all the difference in the world. This book gives concrete steps toward "slaying giants" that we face. It's practical, realistic, and something everyone can do. This book gives us the confidence to believe God is with us, wants us to win, and has in fact already declared us victorious!

HAPPY LEMAN
VUSA National Board Member and
Senior Leader, The Vineyard Church

A quick lesson in life is: If you want to kill giants, learn from the giant killers. Leif Hetland is among the giant slayers of today for sure. Few men live in a constant flow of faith and power as does Leif. His passion for the lost and willingness to go into the darkest places of the world are among the few in the history of Christianity. *Giant Slayers* is a book that will inspire you to live up to who God has called you to be while encouraging you to make the right steps in developing who you are along the way. I highly recommend Leif's new book, *Giant Slayers*.

DANNY SILK
Author, Speaker & President, Loving on Purpose

Honesty. Honesty about yourself and God The Almighty is the key behind *Giant Slayers*. Leif Hetland is honest about his life and that is why the Lord uses him in a mighty way. This book does not focus on the size of the Giants, but rather, who you are connected to when facing a battle. The key is not so much about what you are capable of or what we know, but rather, whom we are with—God!

Giant Slayers will help you to see and act as the Lord does and is a handbook for people who want to move forward. According to Him, nothing is impossible. Leif carries an internal passion to be part of what Papa God is doing and through this book he shares wisdom and insight of how to move forward.

Whether you are facing giants in the safety of your living room or out in the world, when you align with the Father and follow Him onto the battlefield you can be confident you are on the winning team! *Giant Slayers* instructs us how to step out in obedience with God and develop our spiritual muscles in preparation for the battle. Read this book, rest in this book, and I promise you—you will inherit the promises and fulfilment proclaimed!

MARTIN CAVE
Senior Pastor, IMI Church (Stavanger), Norway

I cannot think of a timelier book for The Church right now than Leif Hetland's *Giant Slayers*. Using the familiar story of David and Goliath, Hetland culls a dozen lifechanging principles that—if followed—will truly empower people to live as overcomers. I've heard the call to 'overcome' all my life, but these principles make 'the overcoming life' practical and possible. Knowing God's timing, victory over fear, how to seize one's moments of destiny, how to recognize battles that are not ours to fight, how to make sense of what appears to be tragedies—these are bedrock to a life of purpose and fruitfulness. So many are withdrawing, cocooning, 'checking out.' This book joyously summons us to run to the battle and experience the exhilaration of the power of The Holy Spirit flowing through us in abundance. This book will enable you to dance over the darkness!

STEVE FRY
President, Messenger Fellowship and
Lead Pastor of The Gate Church

Leif is one of my heroes of the faith. He simply carries the love of God. He is slaying giants continually as one who depends fully and completely on our amazing Father. He is paving the way for a generation to run in relationship and intimacy all the while believing that with God all things are possible! This book is a journey on what it looks like to become a giant slayer. I recommend it to all!

TODD WHITE
Evangelist, President and Founder, Lifestyle Christianity

GIANT
SLAYERS

DESTINY IMAGE BOOKS BY LEIF HETLAND

Seeing Through Heaven's Eyes

GIANT SLAYERS

Ground Rules for Overcoming
LIFE'S BIGGEST OBSTACLES

LEIF HETLAND

DESTINY IMAGE® PUBLISHERS, INC.

P.O. Box 310, Shippensburg, PA 17257-0310

"Promoting Inspired Lives."

This book and all other Destiny Image and Destiny Image Fiction books are available at Christian bookstores and distributors worldwide.

Cover design by Eileen Rockwell
Interior design by Terry Clifton

For more information on foreign distributors, call 717-532-3040.

Reach us on the Internet: www.destinyimage.com.

ISBN 13 TP: 978-0-7684-0787-7
ISBN 13 eBook: 978-0-7684-0788-4
ISBN HC: 978-0-7684-1471-4
ISBN LP: 978-0-7684-1470-7

For Worldwide Distribution, Printed in the U.S.A.
1 2 3 4 5 6 7 8 / 21 20 19 18 17

DEDICATION

I dedicate this book to Jennifer, my wife of almost 28 years. "You are my number one supporter and have paid the highest price for me to become a giant slayer. You are the greatest hero in my life. I look forward to the next 28 years as we continue to face the giants in our life and the world together with passion and courage. I love you."

LEIF

ACKNOWLEDGMENTS

I want to thank my assistant Scott Wilson and my team at Global Mission Awareness for your hard work and support. I am very grateful for Dr. Todd Zeiger, Blake Healy and Paul Yadao for your research and insight into this project. My heart is full of joy thinking about the Kingdom Family Movement of giant slayers I am privileged to father. Thank you to Larry Sparks of Destiny Image for his passion to see this project become a reality. To my family: Jennifer, Leif Emmanuel, Laila, Courtney, and Katherine – you are my world and I thank you for your support. Finally, I thank you Holy Spirit, my best friend, for making me look better than I am. You are the best.

Contents

Foreword 17

Introduction. 19

PART 1   Positioning for the Fight 23

RULE 1   Show Up 25

RULE 2   Find the Right Battle. 39

RULE 3   Understand God's Timing. 55

RULE 4   Align with God and Others. 73

PART 2   Stepping onto the Field 91

RULE 5   Don't Lose Heart. 93

RULE 6   Ignore Critics and Face Fear 109

RULE 7   Celebrate Past Victories 127

RULE 8   Seek the Reward 141

PART 3   Taking the Victory. 155

RULE 9   Be Yourself. 157

RULE 10   Bring the Right Weapons 173

RULE 11   Speak Up. 187

RULE 12   Run Forward 203

EPILOGUE A World of Giant Slayers. 221

FOREWORD

Leif Hetland is one of my heroes and has often been one of the key speakers at our global events. He is one of the most, if not the most, courageous ministers I know. I consider it an honor to know him and to be considered one of his friends. I mention this personal knowledge of Leif in order that my statements about him and his new book would carry more weight.

I just finished reading *Giant Slayers: Ground Rules for Overcoming Life's Greatest Obstacles*. It is a powerful book, able to build faith in your life, and if you put into practice the twelve rules for slaying the giants, they will work to create faith in your life to have victories rather than defeats. Leif utilizes the story of David, especially his battle with Goliath, to set the stage for the insights leading to the twelve rules. I love the fact that Leif not only illustrates these rules from David's life, but he shares stories from his own life of the amazing victories he has won when coming against great giants in his life.

Leif's stories are such faith builders, letting us know that the God of David is the God of Leif Hetland and wants to be the great God in our lives enabling us to be able to gain great victories in our lives. Like David and the army of Israel, Leif is going to battle against a giant most of us do not have the courage to attack. As David gave courage to the rest of the army of God as they witnessed David's victory, may the modern-day stories of victory that Leif has experienced create in us a greater faith. Leif helps build our faith to enter the battlefield to fight the giants facing the army of God, the Church today.

But it is not just the stories that are so important; it is the insights Leif lays out for us to enable us to come to the place in our lives to gain these greater victories. My friend Bill Johnson says if you want to kill giants hang around a giant killer. Through reading *Giant Slayers*, Leif is enabling us to be trained by one of the great giant slayers of our day. It is like sitting at his feet as a disciple, gaining the wisdom of a seasoned soldier who explains the strategies necessary to not only survive on the battlefield but to win on the battlefield.

Pick up the book and read it! In your hands you will find a gold mine of wisdom and encouragement. Read and then encourage your friends to read *Giant Slayers: Ground Rules for Overcoming Life's Greatest Obstacles.* In doing so you will be taught by two of the greatest giant slayers in the history of God's people—David and Leif.

RANDY CLARK, D. MIN.
Founder and President of Global Awakening and the
Apostolic Network of Global Awakening

INTRODUCTION

A boy stands in a valley. An army of his countrymen cover the hill behind him. Before him, across an empty plain, towers a famed soldier-giant. He stares at the boy, who wears a basic tunic with a shepherd's bag on his hip and holds a wooden staff and a simple leather sling in his hands. The soldier-giant, who is about nine feet nine inches tall, is clad from head to toe in 125 pounds of bronze armor. He has a javelin strapped to his back, a sword in a scabbard at his waist, and a fifteen-pound spear in his hand. A servant holds his massive bronze shield for him. Insulted by the smallness and seeming inferiority of his opponent, the soldier-giant openly mocks him, assuming his victory will be easy.

The meeting of these two men will decide the battle between their nations. The victor will lead his army to conquest. The loser will be responsible for the defeat and enslavement of his people. They have exchanged verbal threats. Now, the action begins. On the hills on opposite sides of the valley, both armies wait and watch. One feels confident of victory. The other offers up a prayer of hope.

Considering the various decisions that brought him to this conflict, the boy watches his foe, waiting for his moment. Considered too young for battle, he had been left at home to tend the sheep. But that morning he had arrived at the battlefield, sent by his father and carrying a small gift of food for his brothers. His arrival had sparked anger in his brothers, who assumed he had come to gawk at the soldiers. Then, the soldier-giant voiced his challenge, and the boy's heart stirred with indignation. Suddenly, he found himself before the king, pitching his crazy plan. And now, here he stood, facing the giant. So many choices had led to this moment.

As the soldier-giant slowly approaches, the boy watches for his perfect moment, for the brief window in time when he is still out of range of the soldier's weapons but close enough to clearly aim for his target. The first shot matters most; it is his surprise attack. Knowing this, the boy begins to run toward the giant, and as he does he pulls a stone from the pouch, places it in his sling, and expertly slings it at the one part of the giant's body that is not covered by armor. He has done this many times before, but never for such an important cause—never with such monumental consequences.

The soldier-giant is a mountain of a man, the terror of all who oppose him. Every step shakes the ground. His thick armor weighs him down, but he is used to its weight and protection. He is a champion, accustomed to winning, even against the most formidable opponents. He assumes this fight will end quickly—and he is right. Before he can reach his challenger, the boy slings a large, smooth stone, approximately the size of a tennis ball, directly at the giant's face. Faster and deadlier than an arrow, the smooth stone speeds through the air. Before the soldier-giant has time to react, the stone bullet enters his forehead, and he falls to the ground. Within moments, the boy is upon him, drawing the giant's sword and

*severing his head. The battle is over, and the spoils go not to the tow-
ering, many-weaponed giant but to the agile shepherd-boy slinger.*

David and Goliath. It is the most universally well-known Bible story.
People from nearly every culture and demographic reference it as a source
of inspiration and hope. Over and over, it has been held up as an example
of humanity's ability to overcome seemingly impossible circumstances.
The victory of David over Goliath is the hope of every underdog. A man
starts a small business in a field full of well-established competitors, a
young girl overcomes a terminal illness despite the diagnosis, suppressed
people groups transform the cultural and governmental forces that allow
for their mistreatment—our history is full of David and Goliath stories.

These stories inspire us because we live in a world of giants. Some
come knocking on our doors, threatening to tear our lives apart. Others
are far away, guarding treasure and glory, waiting to see who will come
to challenge them. For some, debt is their giant—piling up second and
third notices that they don't know how to answer. For others, it is illness—diagnoses that destroy hope or injuries that put an end to dreams.
And then there's the giant of fear—the paralyzing doubt that sends many
people into long days of procrastination and depression. Some giants take
the shape of various social injustices—exploiting and harming innocent
people. Hunger, disease, poverty, corruption, abuse, deceit, war, addiction,
hate—we live in a world of giants. Some giants threaten us from within
and others threaten us from without.

Fortunately, we also live in a world of giant slayers—ordinary men
and women who overcome the impossible and transform the course of history. We have all heard the story of David and Goliath so many times that
it can be easy to forget what really happened—a giant who had spent his
life learning the art of war was defeated by a shepherd boy. History now
tells us what David became after he defeated Goliath, but on that day no
one yet knew the extent of David's destiny. Though he had been anointed

by Samuel and given a terrific prophetic word about his destiny, he was still a shepherd boy until the day he faced and defeated Goliath. Though we may not feel equal to the task of defeating the giants in our lives, like David, it is our destiny.

David did not defeat his giant by being a warrior of equal strength and size to Goliath. He defeated him by being himself—a shepherd boy. He overcame the great warrior with the slinging skills he had learned while tending sheep. Though he didn't know it, he had been preparing for this battle for many years. The same is true for us. We have everything we need to defeat the giants in our lives. God has already written our victory plan. He has already given us the weapons and skills we need, tucked away in the details of our day-to-day lives. The battle is already ours; all we need is to understand the ground rules.

In this book, through David's story and stories of my own, I provide twelve simple and practical ground rules that will equip us to overcome the obstacles in our lives. Too many destinies have remained trapped in the hands of giants. It is time to stop letting circumstances determine the outcome of our lives. It is time for us to live in all that Jesus died to give us. It is time for us to step into destiny and become the giant slayers we are made to be. It is time to establish God's Kingdom here on earth.

PART 1

POSITIONING FOR THE FIGHT

RULE 1

SHOW UP

Now Jesse said to his son David, "Take this ephah of roasted grain and these ten loaves of bread for your brothers and hurry to their camp. Take along these ten cheeses to the commander of their unit. See how your brothers are and bring back some assurance from them. They are with Saul and all the men of Israel in the Valley of Elah, fighting against the Philistines."

—1 SAMUEL 17:17–19

David is famous for his defeat of the giant Goliath. In the space of one day, he went from unknown shepherd boy to nationally renowned war hero. Just like that, unexpectedly, his life changed. What we love about David is that he was just like the rest of us—an average person living an average life. He had not spent years in the war academy of Israel, training as an elite warrior. He was not a favorite of the king. He was just a normal person showing up for normal life, and one day normal life brought him an extraordinary opportunity.

Yet, we would be wrong if we thought David's lack of military training meant he had no training at all. Normal life was, in fact, the training ground that uniquely prepared David to take down a giant no one else could. As the youngest son, David had received an unimportant job—watching over the sheep. In that day, this task was reserved for the least significant members of the family. It was a job with very little potential for promotion. Though David could have resented this assignment, it seems he instead embraced it patiently and gave it his all. In other words, he learned to serve, and he learned to be faithful with the mundane and inglorious tasks of life.

When the prophet Samuel visited David's father, Jesse, to anoint the future king from among his sons, Jesse did not deem David important enough to have him present at the meeting. Only when God rejected all the others did Samuel ask for and Jesse procure his youngest son. This is the position David held in his family. Even after Samuel anointed him as the future king of Israel, David was sent back to the sheep while his older brothers went off to war. Clearly, David was accustomed to serving—as we see in the start of this story, when Jesse sends him on an errand to deliver food to his brothers. Unknowingly, by being faithful to his father's bidding, David set himself up for his life-changing face-off with Goliath.

In David's example we find this truth: Some of the greatest victories in life begin with being faithful in the small things. Many of our biblical heroes were not doing anything spectacular when God called them. Peter was fishing, Gideon was threshing wheat in a winepress, and David was running an errand for his father. Though these activities seemed unimportant, they were the seedbed for faithfulness. And from those seeds of faithfulness, destiny grew.

Imagine what would have happened if David had not been faithful to his father's will. He could have ignored his task due to bitterness at not being invited to the battle. He could have stayed home due to fear of getting too close to the conflict. He could have seen the errand as unimportant and chosen to do something else instead. When David's father sent him on his errand, the stakes would not have seemed high. He was just bringing his older brothers something to eat. In truth, by being faithful with what was in front of him, David was unknowingly marching toward his destiny. Before he could show up to his battle with the giant, David had to learn how to show up in the little things. He had to cultivate faithfulness.

SHOWING UP EVERY DAY

It is easy to forget how important everyday life is. When work is mundane, when we are given assignments below our skill level, when we feel stuck in the daily grind—we sometimes forget that everyday life is the training ground for greatness. It is where giant slayers are born. David never would have defeated Goliath if he hadn't cultivated faithfulness as a shepherd boy and followed his father's mundane instructions. The truth is, to become giant slayers we first need to learn to show up as shepherds. We have to bring our strength, commitment, and joy to every aspect of our lives.

David's giant-killer instinct sprang up from his personal development in three key areas during his years as a shepherd. He cultivated a *heart* of purity, passion, honor, and obedience. He gave his *hands* to hard work, stewardship, and mastery of skills. And he built *history* with God by encountering Him and experiencing His promises. In other words, he learned to serve from love, not obligation; he learned to pour his heart into every task; and He learned to find his strength and purpose in his relationship with God. David's diligence in daily life prepared him for the challenges of fighting Goliath and becoming king of Israel.

The same will be true for us. We must never forget to do well with what God has already given us. Taking care of what is right in front of us is the best way to get to what is ahead of us. So many people look forward to their destiny and think, *When I get to do that thing I dream of, then I'll give it my all and be amazing.* But that's not how it works. If we don't give it our all now, in the midst of daily life, we probably won't give it our all then, either. The truth is, every season of life has difficulties. Every season of life can, at times, feel boring or frustrating. We will always have the option to give minimal effort or to give up altogether. Showing up in the small things is what prepares us to show up when we face the greater pressures of the battlefield and the throne room. This was true for David, and it's true for us, too.

Whether showing up is as simple as going to work or as complicated as starting a new business, we will never be able to face and overcome our giants until we learn how to show up. Sadly, for this very reason many people never reach their destiny. They fail to cultivate faithfulness in daily life and are, therefore, unprepared for the greatness they are meant for. God does not send us into battles unprepared; He does not send us in where we cannot win. But we must embrace the training process. We must learn faithfulness.

I have learned this in my own life over and over. One of the most remarkable instances of faithfulness leading to a major victory in my life began in the year 2000, when I had an amazing baptism of love experience. As part of this experience with God, I received the spirit of sonship and a spirit of adoption. I also moved into a position of honor toward my spiritual father, Jack Taylor. At the time I did not know how this spirit of sonship and adoption would relate to my calling. I simply knew that God had expanded my heart as a son, and I embraced it as fully as I could. For me, this meant not only growing in my relationship with God as my Father, but also intentionally and consistently leaning into my relationship with Papa Jack. I spent the next five years learning how to truly be a son to an earthly father. Despite our busy schedules, I made it a point to talk to him on the phone daily and receive from him as a father in my life. I still do this, sixteen years later.

After five years of leaning my heart toward my spiritual dad and truly becoming a son to him, a surprising fruit bloomed out of my faithfulness. On a trip to the Middle East, I had the opportunity to meet one of the top Muslim scholars and leaders in the world. When I entered the house to meet with this man, I did not come to him as a Christian leader meeting with a Muslim leader. Instead, God showed me how to act as a son toward this Muslim leader. As a result, over time, this leader began to treat me like a son. The faithfulness I had cultivated in sonship with Jack Taylor enabled me to connect in a surprising way with this Muslim leader. Through my training in sonship, I was uniquely prepared to speak the language of the Muslim culture and give honor to this father. Through sonship, I overcame animosity and created an open door of adoption and respect.

Eventually, when this man passed away, his son—who is a key Islamic figure in his nation and holds a very powerful position—began to call me his brother. As a result, doors in the Middle East began to open before me. Suddenly, I had favor with many Muslim leaders and scholars. In the years since then, this favor has only increased. Now, after sixteen years of daily talking to my spiritual father and positioning myself as a son, some of the leaders of the nations started to honor me as a spiritual father.

This fruit of destiny was hidden in the call to be faithful in sonship. I did not know that something as simple and ordinary as learning how to be a son would open incredible doors for my calling. I did not know it would enable me to befriend and influence many Muslim leaders. All I knew was that God had given me a gift, and I needed to embrace it wholeheartedly and be faithful. Like David, I learned to be faithful as a son, and as a result I was prepared and positioned for my moment of breakthrough. Before David was ready to face Goliath and step into prominence, he needed to be faithful as a son. He needed to be willing, in the natural, to serve his father's dream and live an ordinary life with excellence. Doing so led him toward the moment when he was able to step onto the battlefield and into his destiny.

SHOWING UP TO THE BATTLE

As David so clearly shows us, faithfulness in our daily lives is a skill that will enable us to be who we are made to be. It will enable us to step into destiny and show up to the battle as giant slayers. As children of God, we are designed to destroy the giants in our lives. It's who we are made to be. The ability to overcome is an integral part of our new creation identity. It is our nature to step up and demonstrate the supremacy of Heaven in every situation. But we always have a choice. We get to decide whether we will live in that identity or not. Learning to do so is a process, and faithfulness is our teacher. It develops in us the character—the ability to show up—that we need to face our giants and win. When we know who we are, we will show up for daily life, and by doing so we will prepare ourselves to show up for battle.

We see this in David's life. He chose to show up in daily life—serving his family, working as a shepherd, running an errand for his father. And when that faithfulness took him to a battlefield, he chose to show up in answer to Goliath's threats. There were a hundred moments when David could have chosen to avoid the confrontation with Goliath. Instead, David showed up every time, and he is remembered by history because of it. Showing up is half the battle. We may not win every battle, but we will lose every battle we don't show up to.

I have learned the truth of this in my own life over and over. One giant in particular has taught me the importance of simply showing up, no matter what. This giant entered my life in a sudden and unexpected way, while I was relaxing in a swimming pool. At the time, I was pastoring a small Baptist church in Norway. Every year all the Baptist pastors in the area came together to share fellowship and wisdom. At that gathering, while resting on a bench in one of the many pools at the retreat center conversing with several other pastors, I met my giant.

Without saying a word, for no apparent reason, one of the pastors, messing around, tried to dunk me by jumping directly on to my head. The man, who was a reasonable size, landed square on the top of my head, causing my spine to compress like a spring. Pain shot up my back like lightning, so hot and sudden that my mind went momentarily blank. Later, when asked, the man who had jumped on me couldn't say why he had done what he did. Even the other pastors there were confused as to why it had happened. Something just came over him.

Despite the pain, I tried to attend the meeting later that evening, but as I listened to the speaker my condition began to worsen. My vision blurred and the room began to feel swimmy and uneven. I tried to focus on the pastor sharing at the front of the room, but I began to see double and feel nauseated. I made it back to my room just as the vomiting started. Even with all the lights off and the windows covered, I felt trapped in a whirling blur of pain and confusion. Eventually, the people staying in the room with me decided to take me to the hospital.

The subsequent weeks were filled with uncomfortable tests, prying questions, endlessly increasing pain, and the cold fear of uncertainty. Everything hurt. Light stung my eyes. Lying on my bed in any position caused pain. Standing or moving sent pain bouncing throughout my body. Even looking down to read my Bible caused hours-long migraines. Medication caused as much haziness as it did relief. Even moderate sounds sent a pounding ache through my head. There was no escape.

As this continued, questions and doubts filled my mind: Will I ever play ball with my son again? Will I ever be able to hug my wife without pain shooting up my spine? Will I ever be able to preach again? For six months, I experienced little else but pain and uncertainty. And, worst of all, during this time of confusion and agony I couldn't feel God's presence. I remember the day I hit rock bottom, the day I felt the full weight of despair. I felt mad at God. I felt bitter. Why me? I wondered. I had preached the gospel. I had taken care of my body. What had I done to deserve this? Why should

I lose everything I love in one fell swoop? I will never be able to exercise again. I will never be able to love my wife or my children the way I want to. I will be in torment forever. I felt absolutely hopeless.

Then, in the middle of my sorrow, I felt the presence of God come. He came like a dove resting on my shoulder, a simple and silent weight that brought little more than quiet warmth. He did not bring the answer to all my questions and fears—He simply brought His presence. Slowly, day by day, I learned to focus on His presence. In that season, that was what it meant for me to show up, and many days it took all the determination I had. When I lost my focus on His presence, I could feel it in my body. The pain would start to feel overwhelming again. For this reason, I fought to realign my heart to God's presence every time it slipped away.

In this place of God's presence, my hopes began to come back to life. It took the better part of a year, but I started to learn to live again. I learned to trust the Holy Spirit and partner with Him both physically and spiritually. He taught me how to prepare when I was entering a place with a lot of loud sounds. He gave me the courage to get back to the gym and start from the ground up. He taught me how to worship Him in the midst of pain. Really, He taught me a whole new level of faithfulness. When it seemed like everything had been taken from me, I discovered I still had a choice. I could still show up to the battle in my heart and mind. And this decision to show up, again and again, made all the difference in my life.

Some giants are beaten in a moment, and some we fight for the rest of our lives. My battle against the giant of this injury was not a quick triumph. This is not the last time I will mention my fight with this giant in this book. Though the battle was not won in a day, the day I chose to show up was the day I chose to win. This is the all-important first step in becoming a giant killer. My life would look very different if I had given in to despair, accepted my situation, and decided not to show up to the battle.

We have to choose to show up, no matter what. It really is as simple as that. After the accident, I didn't want to show up to the battle. I wanted to give up. I desperately wanted the pain to end, no matter the cost. At times, going on just felt too hard. But God's presence enabled me to show up one day at a time. I learned how to be faithful and keep moving forward even when I didn't feel like it, even when it took everything in me to hope for victory.

Going to battle against our giants isn't easy. It tests everything in us. In those moments, we are often tempted to give up. After all, giving up is so much easier than fighting. Not showing up for the battle feels like the easy way out. It is an easy way to give up. Instead of quitting, we just never start. But this is a trap. We cannot afford to give up on God or on ourselves. In my battle against pain, I spent too long giving up. It was terrifying to face my situation, but facing my giant was the only way I could start to learn how to defeat it. I did not feel capable of winning, but I knew for sure that if I never faced my giant, it certainly would destroy me.

We all have different giants in our lives. No matter how big or small these giant are, the first step in defeating them is the same—*showing up to the battle.*

THE COST OF NOT SHOWING UP

Obviously, we will lose every battle we don't show up to. We will never defeat our giants unless we first decide to show up to fight them. However, many people still choose not to show up to the battle, in part because they do not know how much it will cost them. When we decide to avoid giants in our lives, the consequences are twofold.

First, we hinder our ability to walk in our destiny. As children of God, made in His image, we are people of destiny. We are destined to overcome giants and to accomplish great feats for the Kingdom of God. When we choose not to show up to the battle, we are, by default, choosing not to pursue our destiny. We are choosing not to be who God made us to be. Doing this changes us. Though we are meant to be more than overcomers, we aren't overcoming anything, and as a result we are not living out our purpose. The cost of this is heartbreaking, as we see in an example from the later part of David's life.

Though he had cultivated faithfulness early in his life and had learned how to show up in his battle against Goliath (and many giants after), at some point David became comfortable. He forgot who he was and stopped acting like the conquering king God had destined him to be. As a result, he decided not to show up to the battle. Instead, *"at the time when kings go off to war"* David sent out his army, but he remained at home (2 Sam. 11:1). While at home, walking his rooftop, David saw a woman bathing and decided he wanted her for himself. This woman, Bathsheba, was the wife of Uriah the Hittite, one of David's mighty men (see 2 Sam. 23:8–39).

While Uriah, David's loyal friend and soldier, was at war, David slept with his wife. And when she became pregnant, David called Uriah home from the battle in hopes of covering up his sin. However, Uriah's warrior mindset prevented him from going home and making love to Bathsheba. When David discovered that Uriah was sleeping at the palace entrance with the servants, David asked him why he hadn't gone home. Uriah said:

> *The ark and Israel and Judah are staying in tents, and my commander Joab and my lord's men are camped in the open country. How could I go to my house to eat and drink and make love to my wife? As surely as you live, I will not do such a thing!*
> —2 SAMUEL 11:11

Here, Uriah demonstrated a true warrior's heart. He was so focused on the battle that he would not allow himself to be distracted. By contrast, David, the man who had shown up and overcome Goliath, made a fatal mistake. He chose not to show up to battle, and as a result he committed the greatest sin of his life. Not only did he steal his friend's wife, but in the end, to cover up what he had done, he strategically planned Uriah's death on the battlefield. The biblical summary of David's life says, *"For David had done what was right in the eyes of the Lord and had not failed to keep any of the Lord's commands all the days of his life—except in the case of Uriah the Hittite"* (1 Kings 15:5). This was David's lowest moment, when he forgot his identity as a giant killer and stayed home from the battle.

When we choose not to show up to the battle, we do so at the expense of our destiny. Like David, we are meant to be giant slayers. We are meant to live victoriously, to move from glory to glory. If we live apart from this destiny, we live apart from our identity. If we move away from our heavenly identity, we are likely to start living in ways that are not heavenly. This is exactly what happened to David, and it is what happens to many Christians who, at some point, decide the battle is too difficult or inconvenient and choose not to show up.

The second cost of avoiding our giants is that we leave undefeated giants in our lives and in the world. In doing so, we actually give them power over us and the people around us. Instead of taking our rightful authority as children of God and serving notice to these giants, we enable their presence by doing nothing. The cost of this decision is not simply personal. It affects more people than we know. Not only do unchallenged giants remain in the land, but the good fruit we are meant to bear never grows. The lack of our destiny means a whole world of people suffers. They need the benefit of what God has put in us, if only we will show up to the battle. This is true of giants that come against us in our personal lives. It is also true of giants that operate at a larger scale and bring oppression to nations and cultures—giants like poverty, racism, and injustice. We live in a world of giants, and it is our job as children of God to kill those giants—both in our personal lives and in the world around us. Many giants roam the surface of this earth waiting for a David to come and remove them. We cannot calculate the cost of leaving those giants undefeated.

We maybe the only solution to some problem

It can be easy to believe the lie that facing our giants is not worth the effort. When we see the enormity of the obstacles at hand, when we feel the pain of pushing through them, it can be easy to become convinced that our struggles will have no lasting effects. Tragically, we usually cannot see how much we have missed out on until we look back at the battles that we did not fight. The greatest rewards often are not apparent until after the battle is won. David knew he would be given money and be allowed to take the king's daughter as a wife if he defeated Goliath. But he did not yet know that this was a victory that would be the foundation of hundreds and hundreds of more victories throughout his life. It would be years before he would know how many victories his battle with Goliath had set the stage for.

Certainly, no one of us can defeat all of the giants in the land, but we are each called and uniquely prepared to battle certain giants. Problems exist that we are meant to solve. We may, in fact, be the only solution to some problems. I am tired of seeing giants rule in people's lives and circumstances. I am tired of seeing giants rule entire parts of our world. God's Kingdom is filled with a vast army of giant slayers. It is time for us to stand up and show up to do our job. The first step is simply deciding to show up in daily life. This is the most important training every giant slayer needs because it cultivates a heart of faithfulness and obedience in us. Then, when the battles come, as they surely will, we must decide to show up, again and again.

We are all in different stages in our journey with God. Some of us have defeated many giants; others are facing their first giant. Some are thriving in life; others are suffering. For some of us, *showing up* looks like leaving the comfort and familiarity of our day-to-day lives in order to pursue a call from God. For others, *showing up* looks like having the courage to get out of bed in the morning. No matter where we are in life, we have a choice. We may think nothing will come of standing up to our giants. The truth is, there is no limit to the good we can bring to the world when, with the Holy Spirit at our side, we step out on the battlefield.

The question is, are we going to show up to the battle or not?

QUESTIONS TO PONDER

1. When you hear the name *Goliath,* what images stir in your spirit?

_____

_____

_____

_____

_____

_____

2. David faced a real giant named Goliath. How do you think this victory affected his life?

_____

_____

_____

_____

_____

_____

3. David's giant had a name. List below the name(s) of your giant(s):

_____

_____

_____

_____

_____

_____

4. Have you missed any of your battles? Was there a time when you didn't show up? Ask the Holy Spirit to show you how you can show up for those battles now and write down what you hear:

_____

_____

_____

_____

_____

_____

_____

_____

DECLARATION

Read this declaration aloud in an authoritative voice, choosing to agree in your heart with these words:

I am created to be a giant slayer. It is part of my destiny on this earth. Even if I don't feel capable, I know the grace of God in my life makes me capable for every battle I face. So, I choose today to show up in every aspect of my life, to live intentionally and faithfully. And I declare, I am a giant slayer!

RULE 2

FIND THE RIGHT BATTLE

Early in the morning David left the flock in the care of a shepherd, loaded up and set out, as Jesse had directed. He reached the camp as the army was going out to its battle positions, shouting the war cry. Israel and the Philistines were drawing up their lines facing each other. David left his things with the keeper of supplies, ran to the battle lines and asked his brothers how they were. As he was talking with them, Goliath, the Philistine champion from Gath, stepped out from his lines and shouted his usual defiance, and David heard it. Whenever the Israelites saw the man, they all fled from him in great fear.

—1 SAMUEL 17:20–24

When a giant presents itself in our lives—like Goliath hollering threats across the valley—before we show up, we must make sure this is a battle we are called to fight. When a battle is personal to our own lives, the need to show up is unquestionable. Only I could be the one to show up in my battle against the injury to my spine and the resulting pain and discouragement. No one could do that for me. However, many of the giants we encounter are giants that affect more than just our personal lives. Like Goliath, they threaten whole people groups. When we see such giants, we must ask ourselves, *Am I called to this battle?*

This is exactly what David did. When he heard and saw Goliath mocking the Israelites, he knew in his heart he was called to fight him. In that day, it was common for armies to settle conflicts through single combat between two champions. This would have been especially advantageous in this face-off between the Philistines and the Israelites. Each army was camped on a hill, with a valley between them. If either army had marched forward to attack, the defending army would have had the high ground, an advantage that probably would have led to an easy victory. Neither army wanted to be the first on the field. It would have been suicide. Enter the Philistine champion, Goliath, a veritable war machine. Daily, he challenged the Israelites to produce a man for him to fight to decide the outcome of the battle.

The problem was, none of the men in the Israelite army believed themselves equal to the task. In all likelihood, none of them could have successfully fought Goliath. After all, Goliath was at least four feet taller than the average man at that time, and he was equipped with the peak of modern battle technology. It was not a fair fight. To the Israelites, the battle looked unwinnable. No one, they thought, could face a man like that—who was both physically insurmountable and carrying the most modern weapons available.

When David arrived and saw the situation, he had a different perspective. This, I believe, is because he was uniquely called to fight Goliath. This was his battle, and he was positioned to win it in a way that the soldiers were not. Here we see that part of showing up is recognizing when we are called to fight a giant. The soldiers of Israel did not have the courage to fight Goliath, but they were not called to. They did not have what it would take. Had any one of the soldiers ventured out onto the field against Goliath, they most certainly would have been defeated. But God had a different plan. He brought David, a brave youth with great skill in slinging, to the battle at just the right moment. God positioned David as a surprise attack against the enemy, and He put the necessary courage and indignation in his heart.

When David heard Goliath's taunts, he recognized him as an enemy of God and as part of his divine assignment. David saw the situation from God's perspective, and he recognized his moment of destiny. He saw that, while the soldiers were helpless to defeat this giant, he had a unique and unexpected skill that could defeat him easily. Because David was connected to God, he knew the right battle to show up for. He recognized his assignment and the divine solution to the problem that God had placed within him. This enabled him to have a victory over Goliath that none of the other soldiers could have had.

Like David, we must be connected to our heavenly Father and the assignment He has given us. This is how we will recognize what battles we are called to and avoid fighting the wrong battles. Unfortunately, many believers get sidelined or distracted by fighting battles they are not called to fight. Some, who do not understand the fullness of the gospel, invest great energy into fighting battles that Jesus has already won on the cross. Others, recognizing a giant in the land, step outside of their destiny in an attempt to fight a giant they are not equipped or called to fight. This would be like Saul trying to battle Goliath. Not every battle is ours to fight. Recognizing what battles we are called to show up for makes all the difference to our destiny.

The surprising adventures of a soldier named Hiroo Onoda illustrate this perfectly.

THE BATTLE THAT'S ALREADY WON

During World War II, Hiroo Onoda, a Japanese soldier, was sent to the Philippines to defend a small island from allied incursion. He and his small band of soldiers fought to the best of their ability, but they suffered several casualties and were eventually cut off from their commanding officers. Isolated and surrounded by their enemies, the group decided to continue their mission and carry out guerilla attacks on any military targets they could find.

They continued their fight until September of 1945 when the Japanese surrendered, putting an end to the war in the Pacific. However, Hiroo and his men were still cut off from any line of communication to their leaders. So, not knowing that the war was over, they continued to fight. The local authorities set up loudspeakers near the jungle where they thought Hiroo and his men were hiding, blasting a message that the war was over and that all of them could go home. Though the soldiers heard the message, they assumed that these messages were simply an attempt to trick them into surrendering. They continued to fight.

Hiroo's soldiers slowly died one by one. Some were killed in combat and others succumbed to the elements until only Hiroo and two of his men remained. One of his remaining men, exhausted and overwhelmed, decided that he would rather surrender to the enemy than spend the rest of his life trying to survive in the jungle. After surrendering and learning that the war had been over for some time, the soldier wrote a note to his remaining comrades, urging them to emerge from the jungle and see that the war was over. These notes were duplicated and air dropped over the jungle. Hiroo and his remaining soldier found the notes, but they assumed the enemy had forced their friend to write the note as a way of tricking them into surrender.

Eventually, Hiroo's one remaining soldier was killed, leaving him alone. He continued to fight for years, still not knowing that the war was over.

Finally, in 1974, a Japanese student, who had heard stories of Hiroo's decades-long fight in the jungle, traveled to the Philippines to find this fabled man. Amazingly, the student was able to find Hiroo and even convince him that the war was now over. However, Hiroo said that the only way he could go home was if his commanding officer relieved him of duty. So the student returned to Japan, tracked down Hiroo's commanding officer (who had long since retired), and brought him back to the Philippines. There, in a military tent and wearing his old uniform, the retired officer officially relieved Hiroo of duty. The soldier, now in his fifties, finally went home.

As the sad story of Hiroo illustrates, it is possible, even from a place of passion and duty, to put all of our time and energy into fighting a battle that is already over. This is a frightening idea. None of us wants to fight a futile or pointless battle. This is why it is essential to marry boldness with a healthy dose of wisdom and good theology when going after the giants in our lives.

On the cross, Jesus defeated many of the giants that have bullied humanity since the Fall. His redemption in our lives is not just for eternal life in Heaven but also for freedom and victory in our lives on earth. Regarding this, Paul told the Galatian Christians, *"It is for freedom that Christ has set us free. Stand firm, then, and do not let yourselves be burdened again by a yoke of slavery"* (Gal. 5:1). In this verse, we find a powerful picture of our spiritual reality as believers. We are already free in Christ. He has won the victory on our behalf. Yet, while we live in this world, we still face giants that try to threaten our victory. Therefore, it is our job to stand firm in Christ's victory and to refuse to allow the enemy to overcome us.

In other words, to avoid fighting a battle that is already won, we need to have a proper mindset about the battles we face. We need to understand that, because Jesus already won the battle against sin and death, we are fighting *from* victory, not *for* victory. We are enforcing on this earth the victory that Jesus already won. This means when defeated giants rear their ugly heads we must use our authority in Christ to command those giants to submit to the victory of Christ. Thus, though at times we still need to engage these giants, we can do so with confidence instead of fear, with pleasure instead of pressure, because the final outcome rests on Jesus' victory on the cross.

This is a reality many Christians have struggled to understand. We need Spirit-renewed hearts and minds to grasp the spiritual reality of what Jesus accomplished on the cross and how it affects our daily lives. In the natural, we might think that if the victory is already won, we should not experience any more battles. For example, if the war against sickness and pain is already won, no one should get sick. Because our current experience is that many people become sick and even die from sickness, many Christians have thought that the giant of sickness is not yet overcome. The Bible tells us just the opposite. The victory Jesus won on the cross includes:

- Forgiveness for our sins (see Isa. 53:5)

- Healing in spirit, soul, and body (see Isa. 53:5)

- The righteousness of Christ and the ability to live righteously in this life (see 2 Cor. 5:21; Isa. 53:11)

- The life of Christ in this life and eternally (see Heb. 2:9)

- The blessings of Christ (see Gal. 3:13)

- The abundance of Christ (see 2 Cor. 9:8)

- Eternal union with God (see Isa. 53:8-9)

All of these are ours, freely given to us through Christ's victory on the cross. Yet sometimes we must fight to defend what we've been given and to establish the victory of Christ in other people and places. The important thing to remember is that when we fight for these realities, we fight in the shadow of a battle that has already been won. Jesus is already on the throne, and His Kingdom is ever growing and expanding to fill the earth. We know the end result will be nothing short of His glory filling the earth and every knee bowing before Him. When we understand this Kingdom reality, we will live and fight from faith and with faith, confident that in Christ we are already overcomers.

THE BATTLE THAT BELONGS TO ANOTHER

Just as we do not want to waste our time fighting a battle that's already been won, we also do not want to risk fighting a giant that is not our assignment. The life of King Josiah, one of the good kings of Judah, shows us the danger of fighting the wrong battle. Josiah sparked a much-needed revival in his nation and caused the people to turn back to God. Yet, he died an untimely death because he sought out a fight with Necho, the king of Egypt. King Necho was on his way to help the Assyrians in their battle against the Babylonians at Carchemish. When Josiah and his army marched out to fight against him, Necho sent Josiah this message:

> *What quarrel is there, king of Judah, between you and me? It is not you I am attacking at this time, but the house with which I am at war. God has told me to hurry; so stop opposing God, who is with me, or he will destroy you.*
> —2 CHRONICLES 35:21

But Josiah did not listen to Necho's warning, and he engaged in a battle he was not called to fight. Because he did not have the calling or anointing of God for that battle, he was vulnerable. His foolishness led him into an unnecessary conflict, and as a result he died a premature

Most often, the battles we fight and the giants we face are put up by the enemy as barriers between our assignment and us. They are obstacles meant to prevent us from being the effective and powerful giant slayers we are meant to be. Because of this, once we understand what our destiny and assignments are, we are better able to identify the obstacles we must overcome and pick the right battles to show up to. Knowing our life assignment when we approach the giants of life will help us avoid wasting our time fighting battles that don't belong to us. For example, because I knew my calling as an evangelist, when I went to Tanzania I was able to avoid engaging a battle on social issues and focus on the spiritual battle.

Our Battle Assignment

We all have an assignment in life, a God-given purpose, yet many people live without a clear sense of what they are called to do. This is not how it should be. God wants us to know our calling and to live with purpose. This is an important part of our identity as giant slayers. To effectively live out our identity as giant slayers, we must know what giants we are called to fight. We must know our destiny. Certainly, discovering the full measure of God's destiny for our lives is a lifelong process, but we can all find where to start. We will not know all the details, but we can discern the general direction of God's call for our lives. We may think of destiny as some grand and far-off reality, but the road to our destiny is often hidden right under our noses—disguised in our passions and desires. Examining what's already in our hearts will help us see our unique calling.

To that end, the following questions will help you identify your area of assignment.

1. What do you love?

Ask yourself: What do I think about? What comes to my mind unbidden? What people group do I feel affection for—the poor, the sick, the hungry, the wealthy, the intellectuals, the atheists, the artists, the governors? What areas of life are most interesting to me—athletics, business, creativity, literature, history, mechanics, nature? What would I gladly do for free?

What we love reveals the gifts God has placed within us. One way to recognize what we love is to consider what we are willing to make sacrifices for. God wants to use each one of us to perpetuate His Kingdom on earth, and He wants to do it through the things we love. Serving Him and fulfilling our calling is not about doing something we hate to do. It's about stepping into our sweet spot and using our passions for His glory.

2.   *What do you see that needs correction?*

What we hate reveals what we are called to correct. We will never change what we are willing to tolerate. And the things we cannot tolerate are the things we are called to change. In all of our lives, there comes a time when we face something so big that it stirs up the warrior in us. Maybe it is an injustice, a people group in need of help, or some other cause. That sense of wanting to "do something about it" is the warrior spirit rising up inside us, showing us our assignment.

Rather than sitting in impotent frustration, let the Holy Spirit teach you how to bring change to places that need it. He wants to partner with you in bringing His loving correction to those areas that have been twisted away from His design.

3.   *What breaks your heart?*

We are called to heal the things that make us cry. Our tears are a window into the calling on our lives. God created passion. It is the heart calling out for heaven's release. Of course, we need to develop skills, wisdom, and maturity to complete our assignments (we discuss this in detail in later chapters), but our assignments begin with our passions.

Do you tear up when you hear about a friend going through a divorce? Maybe you are assigned to bring strength and restoration to families. Does your heart burn when you hear God misrepresented? Perhaps you are destined to bring the revelation of God's goodness to the world. Does your heart break when you hear about orphans? Maybe you are meant to be a father to the fatherless. Jesus was moved by compassion. We, like Him, are destined to bring God's supernatural power to the places that hurt our hearts. Let the Holy Spirit lead you to discover the passions He has placed in your heart. His passion will motivate you to change the world.

This is the key to knowing how to show up for the right battle. Discovering our passions helps us discover our calling, which helps us discern the battles we are called to. Once we have discovered what we are passionate about, we will see clearly the giant (or giants) we are called to fight. Then, we will need to decide how to approach the giants that are blocking the path to our passion. Ultimately, learning to show up for the right battle is a matter of balance. If we are not patient and wise, we will end up wasting our time and energy fighting battles that do not belong to us. But, at the same time, we must also be bold and courageous, choosing to say *yes* to the right battles when we encounter them.

QUESTIONS TO PONDER

1. Have you ever shown up to the wrong battle? Are there giants in your life right now that you know you are not called to fight? What can you learn from these situations?

_____

_____

_____

_____

_____

_____

Knowing your assignment is a critical factor when facing giants. Take the assignment test to determine if you are in the place of proper assignment.

The Assignment Test

1. What do you love? What you love reveals the gifts you contain.

_____

_____

_____

_____

_____

2. What do you see that needs correction? You will never change what you're willing to tolerate. And the things that you cannot tolerate are the things that need to be changed.

_____

_____

_____

_____

_____

_____

_____

_____

_____

3. What breaks your heart?

_____

_____

_____

_____

_____

_____

_____

4. Based on the above answers, what is the Holy Spirit telling you about
    your assignment?

_____

_____

_____

_____

_____

_____

_____

_____

_____

DECLARATION

I am built to be more than a conqueror! I am built to shape societies and bend destinies. I am made to release freedom to captives, bring justice to the wronged, and love to the unlovely. I was built for a cause and equipped to see it done. And I have the wisdom to know what battles are mine. Today I declare that I will show up to the right battle.

UNDERSTAND GOD'S TIMING

David said to Saul, "Let no one lose heart on account of this Philistine; your servant will go and fight him." ...Saul said to David, "Go, and the Lord be with you."

—1 SAMUEL 17:32, 37

David volunteered to fight the giant Goliath because he recognized God's call, as we talked about in the last chapter. He knew this was the right battle for him. But it is possible to fight the right fight at the wrong time. As David listened to Goliath, he not only sensed his calling but also God's timing. He knew it was his moment, and he acted accordingly. This is what caused David to go to Saul and say, "I will go and fight him."

Previously, David had been anointed by the prophet Samuel as the future king of Israel. Yet after he was anointed, David returned to his job watching his father's sheep. It was not yet time for him to be king. In his patience, David displayed great wisdom. It may have been tempting to think about storming the castle, declaring himself the new king, and attempting to depose King Saul. But it was not yet time, and David knew it. Thankfully, David did not try to figure out the timing on his own. He simply waited for his moment.

Not long after, he arrived at the battle with Goliath, which would position him as a leader in Israel's army and connect him closely to Saul's family. David sensed God's timing, and he responded to the call. David was called to be a leader and defender of Israel, and that day, on the field with Goliath, he began stepping into that calling. David's encounter with Goliath was not happenstance. It was a dramatic moment of transition in God's plan for David's life. It was God's perfect timing, and it set David up for so much more than one victory over one giant.

In David's story we see two aspects of understanding God's timing—recognizing the season we are in and recognizing His divine moments when seasons shift and promotion happens suddenly. Both of these aspects of divine timing are crucial to our ability to overcome giants and progress from season to season in pursuit of our destiny.

TIMES AND SEASONS

Not surprisingly, the Bible uses two different words for *time* that embody these two ideas—*Chronos*, meaning "times," and *Kairos*, meaning "seasons." Our lives have different seasons, and often these seasons are earmarked with significant moments of change. If we do not understand this basic principle, we will end up trying to reap during planting season, plant during harvest, run when we should be resting, and rest when it's time to run. Discerning these times and seasons is crucial to our ability to walk out our destiny. If we want to understand how God views time and timing, then we need to understand a little more about these two words.

Chronos—Standard Time

Chronos, which is the root of the English word *chronology,* refers to the general process of time. It represents the day-to-day events that make up our lives. This is time spent getting up, going to work, taking the kids to school, preparing supper—the basics. This kind of time has great purpose in the Kingdom. It is in this kind of time that we build the habits that are an expression of our values. It is in this kind of time that we learn how to practically walk out our victories and revelations in daily life. And it is in this kind of time, as we talked about in chapter 1, that we do the little things that help set us up to succeed in the big things.

Because of this, it is in *Chronos* time, when we are living our most "normal" lives, that we must exercise diligence. We do not earn our right to spend time in the presence of God; Jesus did that for us. But if we are not diligent in the care of that precious gift, we will never become familiar with all that is available to us. Each of us is personally responsible for our own growth. It is in our *Chronos* time that we prepare ourselves for our *Kairos* time.

Kairos—Strategic Time

Kairos refers to the "right" time, the opportune or strategic time, the "now" moments of our lives. These are the moments that are the culmination of our daily thoughts and prayers—when our destiny is obtained or missed. These are the moments when our training and time spent in the presence pay off, or when our lack of diligence and numbness to the Spirit cost us dearly.

While tending sheep, David was living in *Chronos* time. Nothing major seemed to be happening. It was in this kind of time that David watched his sheep, trained with his sling, and spent time in God's presence. Being diligent in his *Chronos* time prepared David to get all that was available in his *Kairos* moment. In one day, he went from tending sheep to killing giants. If we are going to become giant slayers, then we too must learn to be diligent and faithful during our *Chronos* time so that we can recognize and respond to our *Kairos* moments.

RECOGNIZING OUR SEASON

To be faithful with our *Chronos* time, we must recognize our season of life and what God is doing in us through it. Doing so enables us to embrace the process and to be patient as we await our *Kairos* moments. David, it seems, was particularly good at being faithful in his *Chronos* times and embracing the lessons God had for him in preparation for the fulfillment of his calling as king of Israel. He did this not only leading up to his fight with Goliath but also in the seasons that followed.

See, David's victory over Goliath was just the beginning, and the fame and excitement of that victory was relatively short-lived. He did not go immediately from the battlefield to the throne room. Instead, according to most biblical scholars, David was in his early teens when Samuel anointed him to be king of Israel, but he did not become king until he was approximately thirty years old. Even when he became king of Judah, he was unable to unite the whole of Israel until seven years later.

David's journey is a perfect example of how God moves our destiny in a series of divine shifts. Just as David became comfortable and confident with a new season, God would show up suddenly and move him to another level of anointing. David's life shows us what the divine school of life looks like. In school, one studies, learns, and then takes an exam. Life with God follows the same pattern. He teaches and equips us in one season, and then we face a test that, if passed, will launch us into a new season with greater anointing. These tests often come in the form of giants. Though they look like problems, they are really the divine opportunity for breakthrough.

The secret is recognizing our season and embracing the lessons God wants us to learn so that we will be ready when the moment of breakthrough, in the form of a test, stands before us. I've heard people say, "You never fail one of God's tests. You just get to take it over again!" While I do believe God is always willing to give us second chances, I am not that fond of having to retake difficult tests. I would much rather prepare myself to ace every test that comes my way so that there is no delay to the promotion that rests on the other side of that exam.

To help us see better the importance of understanding and embracing our seasons, here I have outlined four of David's major seasons and the lessons I believe he learned during them. In observing the life of someone who was very adept at recognizing God's timing and being faithful in every season, we can learn to see our various seasons not as trials but as triumphs. When we recognize the timing of God, we will see each season and its lessons as His doorway into the next assignment for our lives.

1. Bethlehem—where David learned faithfulness over little things.

When Samuel found David, he was being faithful over natural things—the little things that many would find unimportant. He wasn't in Bible school or the leader of a home group. He was simply serving his father. I doubt it ever occurred to David that he might one day be king of Israel. He modeled the value stated in Zechariah 4:10—"*Who dares despise the day of small things?*" Small beginnings are the seedbed for greatness, as we discussed in chapter 1.

David learned to win wars during his daily routine with the sheep. He did so through killing a lion and a bear. Apart from the practical experience these attacks provided, fighting off the lion and bear taught David to trust God to be his protector, which was the very thing that equipped him to defeat Goliath.

Ironically, in my experience this is often one of the first Christian lessons to be forgotten. Greatness doesn't happen overnight. The daily routine of preparation is what trains us to be ready for the moments of greatness.

The humility that comes from cleaning church bathrooms or setting up chairs for services prepares us for the responsibility of leading thousands. The day of small beginnings prepares us for the day of great victory.

2. *Adullam—where David learned to thrive in his darkest hour.*

After his victory over Goliath, David went to live in the king's court and became a leader in the army. But this seeming promotion was short-lived. Soon, Saul became jealous of David's successes and popularity, and he tried to kill David on six different occasions. Finally, David was forced to flee the luxury of the king's court and hide in the cave of Adullam.

> *David left Gath and escaped to the cave of Adullam. When his brothers and his father's household heard about it, they went down to him there. All those who were in distress or in debt or discontented gathered around him, and he became their commander. About four hundred men were with him.*
>
> —1 SAMUEL 22:1-2

As he sat around a campfire in the cave of Adullam (which means "refuge"), David must have felt confused by his plight. Had he done something wrong? Was he ever going to fulfill the anointing the prophet gave him? What was God doing? This was undoubtedly one of the most spiritually dry seasons of David's life, but God was still preparing him for his destiny. I believe God taught David three key lessons during this dark season. These, in many ways, became the pillars of his kingdom.

First, David learned that the anointing always brings opposition. David's success caused fear and jealousy in the heart of Saul. Saul had lost the anointing, and he saw David as a potential threat to his throne. As a result, David was abandoned by everyone he loved, and it looked like all the favor he had won in the battle with Goliath had been lost. Fortunately, he recognized that his only true source was God.

Second, David learned that God is the only solid anchor. God did not want David's hope and strength to be anchored in the adoration of people, in riches, or in kingly favor. He also didn't want bitterness, self-pity, pride, or the fear of others to be the anchors that comforted and motivated David during his exile. In this dark season, God drew David closer to Him and solidified what David already knew—that God was the one true anchor of his life. In the cave, David learned to make God his refuge.

Third, in the cave, David learned how to be a leader. David had experience as a shepherd and as a warrior. What David did not yet have was experience leading others. But, as he hid in the cave of Adullam, *"All those who were in distress or in debt or discontented gathered around him, and he became their commander. About four hundred men were with him"* (1 Sam. 22:2). God began to bring a group of men to David, a collection of misfits who were in trouble, in debt, and discontented. They may not have been the ideal soldiers, but David had started as something of a misfit himself. He knew the power of God could make a mighty man out of any misfit. So he began to train these men to be giant slayers.

Through this, God taught David how to take the weak and hungry and turn them into the greatest warriors of the age. In his season in the cave, David turned the dregs of society into mighty men of valor. *"They came to David day by day to help him, until it was a great army, like the army of God"* (1 Chron. 12:22 NKJV). In this way, God taught David that, with His help, he could lead anyone.

3. Ziklag—where David learned to take back what the enemy had stolen.

Until David came to Ziklag, he was a man on the run. He had the anointing of a king, but he was running instead of reigning. Then, after David fought alongside the Philistines, the Philistine king offered David sanctuary, giving him the village of Ziklag as a place where his army and all their wives and children could live (see 1 Sam. 27:5–7). For a season, he had a place of refuge, a place he could call home.

However, one day when David and his army of six hundred men returned from the Philistine warfront, they found Ziklag in ruins (see 1 Sam. 30:1–6). While they were away, the Amalekites had raided the village, looted it, burned it, and taken the women and children hostage. David and his men were grief-stricken and angry. In their pain, David's men turned against him and threatened to kill him. After all, it was David who had chosen to leave the city unprotected. This season could have easily become the absolute low point of David's life. He was on the run because the king was out to kill him. His city had been destroyed and his wives and children taken. Now, even his own mighty men were turning on him.

When faced with such devastation and opposition, *"David strengthened himself in the Lord his God"* (1 Sam. 30:6 NKJV). This was perhaps the greatest strength that David had. When things got tough, when his back was against the wall, and even when his own mistakes threatened to bring him to ruin, David always reconnected with God and found the strength he needed to move forward. He responded to difficulty with praise, prayer, and pursuit. Not only did he reconnect with God through praise, but he specifically sought to understand God's timing in his situation, and then he acted accordingly.

First, David praised God. He chose to focus on the promises of God, not the problems at hand. The Bible doesn't tell us exactly how David strengthened himself in the Lord, but I imagine he found a quiet place and sang songs of praise to God. I can see David playing his harp and singing Psalm 34, which he had written when God delivered him from the Philistine King Abimelech:

> *I will extol the Lord at all times; his praise will always be on my lips. I will glory in the Lord; let the afflicted hear*

and rejoice. Glorify the Lord with me; let us exalt his name together.

—Psalm 34:1-3

David had learned the power of praise in the fields with the sheep, and he had seen that power unleashed on the giant Goliath. He knew that praise is the first place to go in any situation.

Second, David prayed. When David went into battle, he called for his generals, but when he needed a word from God, he called for the priest Abiathar.

> *Then David said to Abiathar the priest, the son of Ahimelek, "Bring me the ephod." Abiathar brought it to him, and David inquired of the Lord, "Shall I pursue this raiding party? Will I overtake them?" "Pursue them," he answered. "You will certainly overtake them and succeed in the rescue."*
>
> —1 Samuel 30:7-8

The ephod was the garment of the priest. Each time David sought the Lord, he wore the ephod. This was a prophetic picture of his desire to seek God with all his heart. Even in the most trying of circumstances, David knew he must humble himself before the Lord and seek His direction.

Third, David pursued the enemy in obedience to God's will. In answer to David's prayer, God spoke to David and said, "Pursue for you shall surely overtake them and without fail recover all." This was the revelation of timing that David needed. What had seemed impossible was now completely possible because God had said it was time. Instead of a dark future, David had a new vision of victory. When he acted in obedience to God's timing, he was able to recover all that had been stolen from him and his men.

4. *Baal Perazim—where David learned how to have breakthrough in all seasons.*

Many years later, after David became king over all of Israel, the Philistines heard about it and came in full force against him at Baal Perazim (see 2 Sam. 5:17). *Baal Perazim* means "the master of breakthrough." It would be fair to say that this was David's greatest *Kairos* moment. He was now recognized as king over all of Israel, just as Samuel had prophesied. A divine shift was taking place, and a new test was before him. When we begin to walk in the fullness of our destiny, the enemy always shows up in an attempt to stop us. Each change of season brings a stiffer resistance from the forces of the enemy. The same was true for David. The fact that David had united all of Israel made the country an even greater threat to the Philistines. This was the reason for their attack. If David had lost this battle, his kingdom probably would have crumbled in anarchy. In this moment of divine timing for breakthrough, David did three things.

First, he went to the stronghold (see 2 Sam. 5:17). Spiritual strongholds are where we maintain and then advance against the enemy. When the enemy comes against us, we should go to the place where we are strongest and utilize the gifts God has given us.

Second, David inquired of the Lord (see 2 Sam. 5:19). Instead of acting on his own, which would have been presumption, David stopped what he was doing and asked God for direction. He knew that he could not lead in battle against the formidable army without a strategic plan from God. Because David recognized God's timing, he won the victory that day. However, his enemy did not give up easily. They attacked again (see 2 Sam. 5:22).

Third, David did not repeat past strategy (see 2 Sam. 5:23–25). Once again, David inquired of the Lord regarding His divine timing and strategy. He did not assume the strategy he had used in the first battle applied to the second. Instead of employing past strategies, he sought new revelation from God. This was the key to his final victory over the Philistines. David understood that each new season requires new wisdom and strategies. Breakthrough looks different in every season. This time, God told David He would send the unseen armies of Heaven to overcome the Philistines. David simply obeyed and let God do the fighting. His simple act of obedience released angelic forces to move on David's behalf.

Like few others in the Bible, David modeled for us what it looks like to understand the seasons of life and to live in tune with God's timing. Over and over, he sought God so that he would act strategically, according to the season he was in. He saw his life as a series of seasons and breakthroughs, and he knew that each breakthrough would only come through intimacy with God and awareness of God's perfect timing. If we follow in David's footsteps, we too can learn to be faithful in the seasons of life and recognize the moments of breakthrough so that we can be champions on the battlefields of our lives. We can learn to know the times and be ready when the hour of victory is upon us.

RECOGNIZING OUR *KAIROS* MOMENT

Being faithful to learn what God wants to teach us in every season of our lives prepares us for our *Kairos* moments of breakthrough. Though David did not see all that his battle with Goliath was positioning him for, he did recognize God's timing, and that made all the difference. If we understand, we can value. If we value, we can steward. If we steward, we can multiply. And if we multiply, we can get dominion authority. This is the progression of breakthrough, and it all starts with understanding. David understood. He recognized God's timing and, because he valued it, he responded. Instead of making excuses or ignoring God's timing, he stewarded the moment. As a result, he was able to multiply that breakthrough into the lives of others and eventually to gain authority to create a new culture of dominion over giants for his entire nation.

David's fight with Goliath was about so much more than one battle. It was a moment of divine timing, and it ushered him into a new season in which he would defeat many giants. David's days of battle were far from over. Like David, we too must learn to recognize our *Kairos* moments of destiny. The ability to sense God's timing and act accordingly is crucial to our success as giant slayers.

This has held true in my own life over and over. Often, I have decided to step into certain situations based on my intuitive sense of God's timing, and as a result I was touched by God and used powerfully by Him. In a moment, I was promoted into a new season and new anointing. One of the most remarkable instances of this happened on June 6, 1995. At the time, I was pastoring a church in Norway. Randy Clark was traveling through Norway, and I was scheduled to be his translator at a pastors' meeting. However, I did not want to go, and it seemed like everything in my life was coordinating to make it easy for me to cancel my commitment. This meeting did not feel like it fit into my timing, but it was God's perfect timing.

Several different things, including offense, could have stopped me from showing up at the right time and place to meet the right person and receive the right encounter that was about to transform my life. Thankfully, I did not give in to those pressures, and my wife and I attended the meeting. During the ministry time, Randy came up to me and declared, "You are a bulldozer, and you're going to go into the darkest places in the world where the gospel has never been before." The power behind his words knocked me to the floor, where I stayed for several hours, as I experienced a supernatural encounter with the power and fire of the Holy Spirit. When I got up off the floor, something had shifted in me. It was the beginning of a journey that has lasted for twenty years, so far. In those twenty years, over a million names have been added to the Lamb's book of life.

This entire experience and the resulting fruit hinged on timing. At God's proper time, He connected me with the man who would prophesy my destiny and initiate an encounter with the Spirit that changed me forever. That day twenty years ago was a *Kairos* moment for me that launched me into a new season. It wasn't convenient timing for me, but I needed to adjust my clock to His. I needed to be at the right place at the right time to receive the right touch. Sometimes I wonder, *What if I had not shown up?* I could have allowed the distractions and offenses in my life to make me miss my moment. I am thankful that I listened to the inner voice of the Spirit that day and followed His lead even when it felt inconvenient.

This practice of intuitively sensing the importance of being at a certain place at a certain time has positioned me for many God-ordained encounters and breakthroughs. It is simple, yet it is something we often overlook. In the Spirit, many of our breakthroughs are connected to timing. God's time is moving forward, hour by hour, minute by minute. We simply need to tune our spirits and hearts to the timing of God, listening to His still small voice and following His lead even when it does not make sense and feels inconvenient.

WHAT TIME IS IT?

Sadly, many Christians think they can live by any schedule they choose—either because they think they have their "ticket to Heaven" or because they are unaware of the significance God has placed on their lives. The truth is, *"There is a time for everything, and a season for every activity under the heavens"* (Eccles. 3:1). God does not control every moment of our lives or expect us to follow an inflexible itinerary that tells us what to do at every step. He gives us much freedom. However, He also plants moments of destiny along our paths, and these *Kairos* moments are crucial to our calling. We do not want to miss our moment.

Truly, our ability to manage and understand time and timing can be the difference between being a Pharisee and being a disciple. I have always found the Pharisees to be some of the most tragic figures in biblical history. These men committed their lives to the research and study of the Scriptures. They sought to become familiar with every line and letter of the word, both to live a righteous life and to prepare for the coming of the Messiah. Their entire lives were spent studying the coming of the Savior, and yet somehow they missed Him when He came. They missed Him so completely that they actually plotted against Him.

From a historical perspective, it is not so hard to understand. Israel was under the subjugation of the Roman Empire. They were subject to Roman taxes and Roman laws. They were occupied by an enemy. Many of the prophecies regarding the Messiah described Him as a "conquering king" and a "great deliverer." Many of the Jews were expecting the Messiah to be a great warrior who would come and relieve them of Roman rule. They did not know how to receive their Messiah as a carpenter's son.

Jesus was the breakthrough all of Israel had been waiting for. Yet, most did not pay attention to God's timing, and as a result, they missed their Savior. Not long before His death, Jesus wept over Jerusalem, saying, *"You did not recognize the time of your visitation"* (Luke 19:44 NASB). The Son of God had come to live with them, but only a few had prepared their hearts to recognize Him. The Pharisees and most of the Jews misjudged the times. They expected their Savior to come in one way, and He showed up in another. We cannot afford to make the same mistake.

God orchestrates divine moments of great change and transition in our lives, moments of destiny and promotion. Even when our actions are well intentioned, it is possible for us, like the Jews, to miss these opportunities. This is especially true if we are not faithful to steward the *Chronos* time of our lives and the lessons He has for us in every season. I can think of nothing more tragic than missing a visitation from God because I was not faithful to my season or paying attention to His timing. To avoid this tragedy, we must learn to recognize and understand timing and be ready to receive the opportunities God places in our paths when they arrive. We must not mistake an opportunity for victory as a meaningless obstacle. We have to learn to know what time it is.

In contrast to those who missed their visitation, the Bible tells us of a group particularly skilled at discerning God's timing. The sons of Issachar, one of the tribes of Israel, had *"understanding of the times, to know what Israel ought to do"* (1 Chron. 12:32 NKJV). Their ability to understand and discern the times gave them insight into what action to take. The same can be true for us. Understanding God's timing is often the key to moving into the next level and season of our lives. Because of this, it is essential for us to both *recognize* and *understand* the divine moments God has placed in our lives.

SEIZING THE MOMENT

In 1271, one of the greatest disasters in history took place. Niccolo and Maffeo Polo (the father and uncle of Marco Polo) were visiting Kublai Khan, who at that time was ruler over China, India, and the majority of the East. Niccolo and Maffeo shared the gospel during their visit with this powerful ruler. Kublai Khan was so intrigued by the story of Jesus that he said to these two men, "You shall go to your high priest and tell him on my behalf to send me one hundred men skilled in your religion, and I shall be baptized. And when I am baptized, all my barons and great men will be baptized and their subjects will receive baptism, too. So there will be more Christians here than there are in your parts."

Sadly, Kublai Khan's wish was never fulfilled. It took more than thirty years for missionaries to make it out to China, and even then only three made the journey. Marco Polo, following in his father's footsteps, visited Khan's empire during his travels and discovered small pockets of Christianity throughout the empire. Even without the help and guidance of the missionaries, some had tried to follow Christ.

When Marco Polo returned to inform the church leaders of his findings, suggesting that they send more missionaries immediately, he was met with nothing but opposition. The church leaders were too concerned about protecting their borders from Khan's expanding empire. They thought it would be too much to focus on both defense and evangelism.

It is nearly impossible to imagine what the world would look like now if China had become fully converted to Christianity in the thirteenth century and the East had been given to Christ. It baffles the mind to even consider the magnitude of such a revival. These men missed their divine opportunity, and God's purpose was delayed. The saddest thing is that we will never know what God was planning to do with this potential revival in the East. Of course, it wasn't simple laziness that led to the delay of action to fulfill Kublai Khan's request. Many factors within the structure of the church at the time, as well as the practical limitations of travel in that era, caused the delay and limited the response to the request.

Yet still, I have to believe that if only the church had been preparing itself to fulfill the will of God, history may have been written differently. As this story shows, it is crucial for us to derive our sense of timing and purpose from the Spirit of God. There is no other way to ensure that we do not miss the opportunities He has made available to us. When we train our spiritual senses to be familiar with the timing of Heaven, we will be positioned to overcome. We will learn to embrace every season and be faithful to learn and grow in preparation for our promotion. And when that *Kairos* moment of breakthrough comes, we will recognize it and know what to do.

QUESTIONS TO PONDER

1. What is the difference between *Chronos* and *Kairos*?

_____

_____

_____

_____

_____

2. How do you view the *Chronos* and *Kairos* seasons of your life? Do you view them as connected or independent of each other?

_____

_____

_____

_____

_____

3. Can you describe an event that you now see was a divine shift and you missed God's timing? If so, why did you miss it, and how did it affect you?

_____

_____

_____

_____

_____

4. What specific steps can you take today to further your pursuit of God and His fullness?

_____

_____

_____

_____

_____

_____

_____

DECLARATION

I am thankful for the various times and seasons of my life. I declare that I am one, like the sons of Issachar, who is good at discerning the times and knowing what to do. I am one who knows how to thrive in every season because I have eyes to see what God is teaching me in every season, and I can recognize and understand the Kairos moments of my life.

RULE 4

ALIGN WITH GOD AND OTHERS

Who is this uncircumcised Philistine that he should defy the armies of the living God?

—1 SAMUEL 17:26

David recognized something that every other soldier on the battlefield that day had missed. He recognized that this was not just a battle between nations. This was not just a battle for land or resources. It was also a spiritual battle between the people of God and their enemies. Going out to fight Goliath meant fighting on behalf of God. Of all the people present that day, it seems only David recognized the spiritual realities at work. Thus, while the soldiers showed up for king and country, David showed up for God and His divine Kingdom. He alone saw Goliath's threats not just as a threat to the people of Israel but also as outright defiance of the living God.

David could claim Goliath's threats were an offense against God because of the alliance, or covenant, God had with the nation of Israel.

David could call Israel's army *"the armies of the living God"* because God had promised to stand by Israel as His people. When Moses led the Israelites out of Egypt and to the foot of Mount Sinai, where they received the Ten Commandments, God engaged the new nation in a covenant in which they agreed to serve Him and obey His commands and He agreed to protect and prosper them. In David's day, this covenant—what we now call the Mosaic Covenant—was still in effect. When an enemy came against Israel, that enemy came against God Himself. This should have been obvious to all of the Israelites, but it seems that only David took it seriously. The army's leader, King Saul, had become proud and rebellious toward God, and God had rejected him as king (see 1 Sam. 15:23). It is not surprising, then, that Saul did not think to align himself and the armies of Israel with God's covenant promises.

Fortunately, David saw things differently. He saw Goliath for what he was. By referring to him as an *"uncircumcised Philistine,"* David was pointing out Goliath's lack of relationship with God. Ever since the days of Abraham, the Israelites had seen circumcision as a physical symbol of their spiritual covenant with God (see Gen. 17:10–14). Goliath existed outside of the covenant, and therefore he was an enemy of God. In light of this, David was shocked that the armies of Israel, who were the children of the living God, would allow a man who had no covenant with God to defy and insult them.

Unlike his countrymen, David knew what it meant to be in a covenant with God. He understood that God is a God of justice, a God who is faithful to fulfill His promises. To David, this was not just a nice idea. It was his reality—so much so that he was willing to bet his life on it. Shocked and perhaps even offended that his countrymen had forgotten their covenant with God—David stepped into battle based on his spiritual alignment with God.

ALIGNING WITH GOD

As we prepare to fight the giants in our lives, we cannot overlook the importance of alignment. Like David, if we want success we need to rely on our connection to God and our status as His children. David lived under the Mosaic Covenant, or old covenant, which the New Testament calls an inferior covenant. *"The covenant of which* [Jesus] *is mediator is superior to the old one, since the new covenant is established on better promises"* (Heb. 8:6). Now, in Christ, we have received a better covenant with better promises. What that means is that everything David received through his alignment with God under the old covenant—and so much more—is available to us through our alignment with Christ and His new covenant.

While the old covenant was conditional on Israel's obedience to the Law, the new covenant is based on our faith in Christ. It is not based on anything we might do to receive it, but instead we receive it as a gift because of what Christ has already done on the cross. Some Christians mix the covenants, thinking they are in danger of losing God's blessing if they make a mistake or do not work hard enough. This is a wrong understanding. We are aligned with God through faith in Christ, and we live in His Kingdom by grace. This is crucial to our ability to successfully fight the giants in our lives.

When we understand this, our awareness of our new covenant alignment with God will give us two important keys to victory:

1. Listening to His Voice

First, awareness of our alignment with God reminds us of the importance of listening to His voice for direction and strategy in our battles. First comes the alignment; then comes the assignment. We can be in the right place at the wrong time, or we can be at the wrong place at the right time. Both will end in disaster. In chapter 2, we talked about discerning our calling so that we know what battles are ours to fight. And in chapter

3, we talked about discerning God's timing for our battles. Just as we must listen to His voice to arrive at the right battle at the right time, so too we must listen to His voice to discover the right strategy. (We will talk in more detail about strategy in chapters 9 and 10.) The Bible is full of stories of individuals who knew their divine calling but who relied on their own wisdom for how to go to battle. We do not want to fight giants in our own wisdom.

Instead, we must follow David's example. We must lean into our alignment with God by listening to His voice. In his battle against Goliath, the passage does not tell us much about David's inner dialogue or how he received his strategy. But we know from his writings in the Psalms that he maintained a very intimate relationship with God. It is reasonable to believe that God directed David in his strategy. We find a clearer example of this very sort of alignment in later battles in David's life. On many occasions, as David prepared for war, he *"inquired of the Lord"* and received strategy for victory (see 1 Sam. 23:4; 30:8; 2 Sam. 2:1; 5:19, 23). Likewise, when the nation of Israel suffered from a famine for three years, David asked God for wisdom regarding the famine. In response, God showed him the cause of the famine and the way to lift it (see 2 Sam. 21).

In John 6:1–12, Jesus also demonstrated the need to listen for Heaven's strategy for the problems we face. A great crowd of people had followed Jesus onto a mountainside to hear Him preach. However, they had not brought food with them, and the people needed to eat. Jesus had a plan, but to test His disciples He asked, *"Where shall we buy bread for these people to eat?"* (John 6:5).

Philip, clearly feeling overwhelmed by the dilemma, answered, *"It would take more than half a year's wages to buy enough bread for each one to have a bite!"* (John 6:7).

Then Andrew spoke up: *"Here is a boy with five small barley loaves and two small fish, but how far will they go among so many?"* (John 6:9).

While both Philip and Andrew looked at the problem from a natural perspective and saw only impossibility, Jesus looked at it from a heavenly perspective. He recognized that the problem could not be solved naturally, but He knew His Father always has a solution. Jesus tapped into Heaven's strategy, and He multiplied the food.

> *Jesus said, "Have the people sit down." There was plenty of grass in that place, and they sat down (about five thousand men were there). Jesus then took the loaves, gave thanks, and distributed to those who were seated as much as they wanted. He did the same with the fish.*
>
> —JOHN 6:10-11

God's strategy is always the best. No matter what problems or giants we face, God knows what to do. No giant is too big for Him, and as His children all we need to do is listen for His direction, confident that when we ask for wisdom, He will give it (see James 1:5–7).

In 2013, I had the honor of visiting Pakistan for several strategic events. After a grueling journey, we arrived in Lahore in the middle of the night. The arrival was a culture shock with sounds and smells as all senses were completely overwhelmed with the contrast to where I had just come from. Exhausted, I tried to get some sleep before our busy schedule began, but just as I began to sleep the first call to prayer began making it impossible to sleep. A little irritated due to exhaustion, I decided to switch on the television to try and watch some news, but instead I came across some Arabic and Urdu teaching on the national channels. Despite having seen this one particular teacher for several years on the television, this time as I watched something was different.

As I watched his teaching, I sensed the Holy Spirit say, "Do you see that man? I want you to meet him today." I sat there in the middle of my fatigue thinking that there is no way I would know how to connect with this teacher, let alone meet with him. It would be like watching television back home and deciding to try and meet Oprah. It seemed impossible. Finally, I asked my coordinator to attempt to set up a meeting—an attempt that returned with a resounding *no*. I then heard the Holy Spirit say, "I did not ask you to *try* to meet him. I asked you to meet him."

It was at this point that I knew God was going to invite me into something that I had not yet understood. I heard the Holy Spirit ask me, "When you see this man, what do you see?" As I listened to God, I realized in this moment that this was an invitation like that depicted in scripture—when I am looking at Saul, can I see the apostle Paul? When I look at Jacob, can I see an Israel? When I look at someone, am I seeing them based upon their history or their destiny? It was with this revelation that my eyes were opened to respond to the Holy Spirit's question with "I see a man of peace. I see an Ambassador of Peace." God took me into the future to show me what this man was going to be, not who he was now.

Based upon this revelation, I decided to create and award this leader the International Peace Award to be presented by my organization. I had my coordinator arrange for a sculpture to be inscribed with the accolade and the recipient's name and we traveled to his headquarters. From having listened, we were now walking in God's plan, and the barriers were removed, doors were opened, and we were miraculously allowed access to honor this man. I now had the opportunity, through covert language, to honor this man as God sees him and engage in a relationship that has continued to this day—a relationship that has the ability to impact the lives of sixty million people every day. By listening to God, I was able to hear what He was hearing, see as He was seeing, and then do what He wanted to do.

In all this we see the importance of alignment. We have a covenant with God, but if we do not align ourselves with our covenant by listening for His direction, we risk disaster. We must first align ourselves with

Heaven, setting ourselves to be in sync with God and our relationship with Him. From that place of alignment, we will not only know our assignment, but we will also receive wisdom regarding timing and strategy. This will enable us to approach our assignment well and to successfully enforce Christ's new covenant victory wherever we go.

2. *Remembering His Promises*

Second, awareness of our alignment with God reminds us of the many promises God has given to us as part of the new covenant. We cannot afford, like David's countrymen, to forget who God is and His power in our lives. No matter the circumstances, no matter how bad things appear to be, we must remember that we have a covenant with God and that God's promises are always true. In fact, the Bible tells us that God is *the truth* (see John 14:6). It is part of His character and identity. He embodies truth. Thus, regardless of what we may experience, aligning ourselves with God means clinging in faith to His promises as a greater reality than our circumstances.

For example, some Christians believe sickness is sometimes God's will for our lives. They base this belief on their experiences with sickness. They have prayed for people who were ill, and those people did not get better. God is all-powerful, so that must mean God wants those people to remain ill. Or so their reasoning goes. In this way, they allow their experiences to create their beliefs instead of allowing their beliefs to shape their experiences. The Bible is full of promises regarding God's desire to heal all sickness. How we position ourselves in relation to the promises of God has a huge impact on our ability to successfully defeat giants.

To be giant slayers, we must be like Abraham, the father of faith, about whom Paul wrote:

> *Yet he did not waver through unbelief regarding the promise of*
> *God, but was strengthened in his faith and gave glory to God,*

being fully persuaded that God had power to do what he had
promised. This is why "it was credited to him as righteousness."
—ROMANS 4:20-22

Not only does God have the power to do what He has promised, but He is righteous and faithful to keep His promises. Faith means holding to this truth, even when we do not yet see the fulfillment of His promises. Doing so aligns us with God and our covenant with Him. In this way, we take our stand against our giants by the strength of God's promises.

The Bible contains hundreds of promises for our lives. Following is just a sampling of the promises of God for all who follow Him:

- If we seek for God, we will find Him (see Deut. 4:29; Luke 11:9–13).

- God protects us (see 2 Thess. 3:3; Ps. 121).

- God's love for us will never fail (see Rom. 8:35–39; 1 Cor. 13:8; 1 Chron. 16:34).

- God blesses all who believe in Him and delight themselves in Him (see Eph. 1:3; Ps. 1:1–3).

- God gives salvation and eternal life to all who believe in His Son, Jesus (see Rom. 1:16-17; John 3:16; 4:14).

- All things will work out for good for God's children (see Rom. 8:28).

- God promised He will comfort us in the midst of our trials (see 2 Cor. 1:3-4).

- We have received new life in Christ and now live as new creations in His image (see Rom. 6:4; 2 Cor. 5:17).

- We possess every spiritual blessing in Christ (see Eph. 1:3).

- God will finish the work He has started in us (see Phil. 1:6).

- God gives us peace when we pray (see Phil. 4:6-7; Rom. 8:6; 15:13).

- God will supply all of our needs (see Matt. 6:33; Phil. 4:19).

- God gives us rest (see Matt. 11:28–30; Heb. 4:9-10).

- God gives us abundant life (see John 10:10; 3 John 1:2).

- God gives us supernatural power to do the works of the Kingdom (see Acts 1:8; 1 Cor. 4:20).

We cannot afford to view these as idle or meaningless. Instead, we must stand on these promises and set them as the standard for our lives in Christ. Otherwise, it will be too easy to allow giants to come in and steal our inheritance in Christ. The promises and the victory are already ours, through Christ, but the giants do not want to admit it. They try to intimidate us with lies about ourselves and God. Only when we hold on to what the Bible says about who God is and what He has given us will we be able to stand up and overcome. Like David, we must bravely stand in defiance of the threats of the giants in our lives.

David's brief battle with Goliath was about to begin; David declared, *"All those gathered here will know that it is not by sword or spear that the Lord saves; for the battle is the Lord's, and he will give all of you into our hands"* (1 Sam. 17:47). In other words, David entered battle declaring his alignment with God and his trust in God as the one who would bring the victory. It is essential to remember, like David, that the battle belongs to the Lord. The giants of life are not just obstacles for us; they are places where we are meant to enact the will of God on the earth.

We must approach every battle of life with the knowledge that the battle already belongs to the Lord. Knowing this will completely change the terms of every conflict. It will cause us to approach battle in a different way—with a heavenly perspective. This alignment with Heaven will be the difference between victory and defeat.

ALIGNING WITH OTHERS

To successfully fight our giants, not only must we align with God, but we must also align in covenant relationships with other people. After his victory over Goliath, David began to serve in Saul's army, and during that time he became close friends with Saul's son and heir, Jonathan:

> *And Jonathan made a covenant with David because he loved him as himself. Jonathan took off the robe he was wearing and gave it to David, along with his tunic, and even his sword, his bow and his belt.*
>
> —1 SAMUEL 18:3-4

It was no small thing for the heir to the throne to give his robe, tunic, sword, bow, and belt to David. It seems that Jonathan recognized the call to the throne on David's life and pledged himself to be loyal to him, even though it meant giving up his right to the throne. As a result, when Saul attempted to kill David, Jonathan protected and assisted him (see 1 Sam. 19-20; 23:15–18). In David's battle against Saul, he needed not only alignment with God but also alignment with covenant friends—first Jonathan, and later his band of mighty men who fought alongside him in the wilderness (see 1 Sam. 22). The same is often true for us. Often, we cannot defeat the giants in our lives on our own. We need the support found in covenant relationships with spiritual family.

Several years ago, I experienced the power of covenant relationships helping me overcome a personal giant. After a ministry trip to the Philippines, I came home feeling very tired and ill. I felt dizzy and weak, and I had lost twenty-five pounds. Though I did my best to rest, even breathing was exhausting. When I went to the hospital, a CAT scan revealed that I had a severe case of double pneumonia, but that wasn't all. The doctor also found a baseball-sized tumor near my lungs. Further testing revealed that this was a parasitic tumor that was literally sucking the life out of me.

The news came as a complete shock. Other than the sudden illness at the end of my trip, I had been feeling fine. How could a tumor have been growing in me all this time? The spiritual and physical exhaustion was so severe that I hardly remember all the tests that the doctors performed on me. The only option was to operate immediately. Feeling very discouraged, I sent word to my close friends and colleagues from around the world. Immediately, I received an enormous outpouring of prayer and encouragement. People sent letters and emails and made phone calls. They had their congregations pray and sent me prophetic words about the plans God had for my future. I was completely blown away.

In particular, one of my spiritual sons, Paul Yadao from the Philippines, flew to be with me before the surgery. He soaked me in the presence of God for hours at a time. At one moment, as I received of God's presence and peace from him, Paul told me, "You're going to live."

"How do you know?" I asked him.

"Look in the mirror," he said.

When I looked in the mirror, instead of the pale face I had grown accustomed to seeing since the start of the illness, I saw a face that glowed. At that moment, something shifted in my heart. In one night, I went from being certain that I was going to die to certain that I was going to survive. I was so full of faith that I even paid the doctor to do one more scan right before the surgery. The scan revealed that the tumor had shrunk by one inch in diameter. We still went ahead with the surgery, but I felt nothing but peace as I entered the operating room. When the doctors removed the tumor, they discovered that it had become nonmalignant. This was a great miracle, and I believe it happened in large part because of my alignment in covenant with spiritual family.

There is so much power in covenant. In my time of unexpected pain and confusion I was saved by the encouragement of my covenant relationships. My close friends and family reminded me of the covenant I had with God. They reminded me of all the promises that God had made about my life and that no tumor could ever undo them. My dear friend Paul helped me to rest and abide in God's presence, even in the midst of the battle, and as a result, the enemy's attack was turned into a season of healing and spiritual upgrades in my life. It was not just the doctors and nurses who took care of me but also my spiritual family, who know how to pull from Heaven and change atmospheres. Because they fought on my behalf in the spirit realm, tremendous transformation took place—both in my body and in my heart—in the five months between when I was diagnosed and when I recovered.

During that season, as all of the love, prayers, and prophetic words poured in, I was reminded of a story a friend of mine once told me. He said redwood trees, though they are some of the tallest trees in the world, do not have especially deep roots. Alone, a redwood tree would be in great danger of falling over. But redwoods tend to grow close to one another, and under the soil their roots bind together, adding strength and support. When a storm comes through, the roots tighten around each other, making redwood forests some of the most steadfast in the world. This is a beautiful picture of what covenant relationships and alignment with one another can do for us.

We are designed to bind to one another and support each other when we face challenges. Some people think they are better off alone, that connection is too messy and painful. The opposite is true. We are designed for connection, just like redwood trees. We are built for covenant, not only with God but also with one another.

FROM CONVENIENT TO COVENANT

In our modern world, we have lost much of the original understanding of covenant. Many people find it easy to slip in and out of relationships at their convenience. But our relationships should be about more than just "getting along." This is true of our relationship with God and our relationships with others. Our connections to others should never be about what others can do for us. Instead, true commitment creates an atmosphere where healthy relationship can thrive. This is God's desire in His relationship with us, and His desire for our relationships with one another. When God sent His Son to die, making us free from the law of sin and death, He gave us salvation as a free gift. In this free gift is a promise to accept us for who we are. By doing this, He opened the door for us to step into covenant with Him. This is what alignment with Him looks like.

Likewise, in our relationships with one another, when we build a relationship on the foundation of covenant we create an environment of safety and security, a place where we are free to be as we truly are. Marriage is a powerful form of covenant, but family relationships and friendships can also hold covenant commitment. This is so contrary to how the world does relationships, but it is what we were made for. Covenant is safe and secure because it is solid. It is not easily broken. I cannot say I have made a covenant with my wife and then go hang around with other women. If I did so, my covenant would mean nothing. Covenant creates boundaries that are designed to protect that which is most important. Covenant says, "I am with you for the long haul, no matter what." That's what God says to us, and it's what we get to say to one another.

Unfortunately, many of us have allowed our covenant relationships to become relationships of convenience. This is a costly choice that will undermine the power of our connections. If we abandon one another at the first sign of trouble, what does our covenant mean? If we abandon God at the first doubt or unanswered question, what does our covenant mean? Our covenants with God and each other should compel us to protect our connection.

David knew he had a covenant with God. And based on that covenant—his commitment to God and God's commitment to him—David volunteered to fight the giant who was mocking God's people. He was quick to stand by God, and he was confident God would stand by him and bring him the victory over Goliath. This sort of relational alignment—with God and with one another—is a key to not only defeating the giants in our lives but to becoming giant slayers for the Kingdom of God.

We are meant to be the ones who charge to the aid of our friends, the ones who show up when life is at its most desperate. We are made to be those who show up in the darkest corners of the world, carrying the light of God in both hands. Our commitment to God should lead us to come against the giants that try to steal from His children. And God's commitment to us should give us the courage, boldness, and confidence to know He has given us everything we need to defeat the giants we face.

QUESTIONS TO PONDER

1. David knew God had made a covenant with Israel. This compelled him to face Goliath. What promises has God made about the giants in your life?

_____

_____

_____

_____

_____

2. Reread the list of biblical promises and hold each one up to your life. Which promises stand out the most to you? Are you experiencing the fullness of God's promises? Do you need to remind yourself of these promises? Do you need to defeat a giant standing in the way of these promises? Do you need to declare these promises over your life? Let the Holy Spirit guide you to the promises that you need most.

_____

_____

_____

_____

_____

3. Who would you want to come around you during a time of crisis? Who are your covenant friends?

_____

_____

_____

_____

_____

_____

4. Read Matthew 16:16–19 and think about Jesus' reaction to Peter's declaration of personal belief. If Jesus asked you the same question, what would you say? Are you building your life around your firm belief that Jesus is the Lord of your life?

_____

_____

_____

_____

_____

5. Find a quiet place and listen to the Holy Spirit for a few minutes. What personal promises is He declaring over your life?

_____

_____

_____

_____

_____

_____

DECLARATION

I come into alignment with God and His new covenant right now, and I declare that I will act according to His will and calling. I commit myself to the spiritual family God has given me. I declare that I will live in covenant with them, and I will be a blessing to them.

PART 2

STEPPING ONTO THE FIELD

RULE 5

DON'T LOSE HEART

Whenever the Israelites saw the man [Goliath], they all fled from him in great fear. ...David said to Saul, "Let no one lose heart on account of this Philistine; your servant will go and fight him."

—1 SAMUEL 17:24, 32

As David arrived at the battlefield, he heard Goliath's threats and witnessed the great fear that had pervaded the Israelite army. Trained and war-hardened soldiers fled from the giant in great terror. Even Saul, the king and leader of the army, who had won great victories for Israel in the past, had lost heart at the threat of Goliath. Into this environment stepped David, who was not an experienced warrior, but who had an unshakable heart. And it was he who won the victory.

The heart matters. It is the essence of who we are, and it determines how we will respond when the pressure is on. As Jesus said:

A good man brings good things out of the good stored up in his heart, and an evil man brings evil things out of the evil stored up in his heart. For the mouth speaks what the heart is full of.

—LUKE 6:45

The Israelite army may have looked formidable. They may have boasted of their courage. But their hearts betrayed them when Goliath challenged them. Unlike the Israelite soldiers and king, David had a heart that could not be beaten down, even when everyone around him had already given up. This gave him the inner strength needed to face the giant everyone else feared. David was just a shepherd boy, but the quality of his heart gave him the inner resources he needed to defeat Goliath and then, eventually, to ascend all the way to the palace. Truly, there is something about the condition of our hearts that turns us into giant slayers. The tenacity of our hearts determines the probability of our victory.

THE HEART SHINES BRIGHTEST

David was the youngest of his brothers. This meant a great deal in ancient culture. The line of favor and responsibility always started with the oldest and went down from there. It was a massive upset of social norms when the prophet Samuel anointed David rather than one of his brothers. But God does not make His choices based on social norms; He makes them based on the condition of our hearts. God picked David over all his brothers for exactly this reason, and it shocked David's father, his brothers, and David himself. Even Samuel, who came to do the anointing, was surprised by God's choice (see 1 Sam. 16:6–13). But God was clear about His priorities:

Do not consider his appearance or his height, for I have rejected him [Eliab]. *The Lord does not look at the things people look at. People look at the outward appearance, but the Lord looks at the heart.*

—1 SAMUEL 16:7

We all have different ways of measuring worth. Some people judge others by their looks. They ask, *Who is the most beautiful? Who has the biggest muscles? Who has the whitest teeth?* Others judge based on accomplishments. According to this standard, what matters most is how much one has done and how prestigious one has become. Those who judge by this standard ask, *Who has the most degrees? Who has the most experience? Who has the most money? Who runs the biggest company?*

Some Christians even use spiritual accomplishments to measure the worth of others. Such people might make comparisons like: *Who has led more people to the Lord? Who has seen the most people healed when they pray? Who has the largest church? Who spends the most time praying and reading the Bible or attending church services?* However, all of these questions are useless in determining true worth. To those who judged by appearances, Jesus said, *"You are the ones who justify yourselves in the eyes of others, but God knows your hearts. What people value highly is detestable in God's sight"* (Luke 16:15). The true quality of a person is determined by the heart.

God, *"who knows the heart"* (Acts 15:8), does not measure using any of these scales. He measures by looking at the heart. Chances are that someone with a good heart will be successful in any number of areas, but success exists on the outside and is not a perfect indicator of what is on the inside. Eventually the overflow of the heart surfaces and can be seen outwardly, as Jesus said, but often a person's inward faithfulness (or lack of it) is hidden for a season. Accomplishments can be the result of performance, strife, fear, and even anger. For this reason, the motives behind our good deeds are more important than the deeds themselves.

Samuel was surprised when God revealed Jesse's youngest son as the future king. He could not see what God saw, but eventually the quality of David's heart was revealed by his actions on the battlefield. When everyone else shrank back, David bravely trusted in God.

QUALITIES OF A STRONG HEART

Like David, we are called to be people who do not lose heart when facing the giants of life. While the Bible lists many traits of those who are good in heart, three specific traits stand out in the story of David and his ability to succeed as a giant killer. David did not lose heart because his heart was courageous, his heart burned for God's justice, and his heart was unbreakable.

A Courageous Heart

By volunteering to fight Goliath, David displayed incredible courage. The Bible does not tell us whether David felt afraid. Most likely, he felt at least a little fear. But regardless of what he felt, he chose to fight. As someone once said, courage is not the absence of fear but the decision to act in spite of fear. David knew that defeating Goliath was more important than any fear he may have felt. He was willing to risk his life for the cause. Not only that, but he was confident that God was on his side. It is this trust in God that is the source of a courageous heart. David shows us this in Psalm 27, where he describes his unwavering courage:

> *The Lord is my light and my salvation—whom shall I fear?*
> *The Lord is the stronghold of my life—of whom shall I be*
> *afraid? When the wicked advance against me to devour me, it*
> *is my enemies and my foes who will stumble and fall. Though*
> *an army besiege me, my heart will not fear; though war break*
> *out against me, even then I will be confident.*
>
> PSALM 27:1-3

The brazen courage and confidence in these words is rooted in David's unflinching trust in God. As the psalm goes on to explain, David knew, because of his intimate relationship with God and his hunger to be in God's presence, that God would keep him safe. The very presence of God was his protection (see Ps. 27:4-5). In light of this, David ends his psalm with this manifesto of hope: *"I remain confident of this: I will see the goodness of the Lord in the land of the living. Wait for the Lord; be strong and take heart and wait for the Lord"* (Ps. 27:13-14). David knew how to take heart, how to strengthen his heart in God's promises. This is what made him unique on the battlefield. As a worshiper and lover of God, he knew God would protect him. And this confidence filled his heart with courage.

This sort of courage should be a trait of all believers because God has put His Spirit in our hearts as a promise of what is to come (see 2 Cor. 1:22). We live with the promise of His goodness, and this promise should fill us with great courage. Jesus, as He talked to the apostles about what it would be like after His death, told them, *"Peace I leave with you; my peace I give you. I do not give to you as the world gives. Do not let your hearts be troubled and do not be afraid"* (John 14:27). In Jesus, we find the peace that empowers courage.

That is exactly what happened to the apostles after Jesus' death and resurrection. Though previously they were cowardly, His Spirit in their hearts emboldened them so much that even their enemies noticed.

> *When they saw the courage of Peter and John and realized that they were unschooled, ordinary men, they were astonished and they took note that these men had been with Jesus.*
>
> —ACTS 4:13

The apostle Paul also testified to the courage of Christ in his heart. He confidently believed that in the moment of battle he would have the courage needed to glorify Christ in his actions, whether he lived or died (see Phil. 1:20). The early believers faced great persecution, and many gave their lives for the gospel. It is no surprise, then, that courage was a theme among them. They knew, like David, that no matter what giants they faced, God would strengthen their hearts. Their intimacy with Jesus and their belief in His promises enabled them to declare, *"Since we have such a hope, we are very bold"* and, *"Since through God's mercy we have this minis-try, we do not lose heart"* (2 Cor. 3:12; 4:1).

The same strength of heart is available to each one of us. No matter what we face, God says to us, like He said to Joshua, *"Be strong and coura-geous. Do not be afraid; do not be discouraged, for the Lord your God will be with you wherever you go"* (Josh. 1:9). This reality will fill our hearts with courage.

A Heart Burning for Justice

The second trait of those who do not lose heart is a passion for God's justice. People with good hearts are motivated by love and compassion. They fight for the sake of others, and they hunger to see God's will made manifest on the earth. We see this in David's initial response to hear-ing Goliath's threats. He immediately became personally affronted. His heart would not allow him to accept the giant's mockery or the threat to his people.

David began asking those nearby about Goliath and about what reward would be given to the man who fought him. Hearing this, his older brother reprimanded him harshly, accusing him of having wrong motives. In response, David said: *"What have I done now? Is there not a cause?"* (1 Sam. 17:29 NKJV). In these simple words, David once again revealed the purity of his heart. The accusations of his brother held no sway because David knew his own heart. It is possible that a young man, especially one who was not invited, would come to a battle seeking glory or looking to see a little action, but David was not motivated by such things. His cause was pure because his heart burned to see God's justice. When he was confronted by the giant, David's heart gave him a cause. He took personal responsibility for the giant and vowed to defeat him.

Like David, each one of us has been given a cause, and chances are there are giants standing in the way of our causes. God is a God of jus-tice, and a large part of our destiny on earth involves bringing His justice to the people and situations that need it. We see this in the description of God's throne in Hebrews: *"Your throne, O God, will last for ever and ever; a scepter of justice will be the scepter of your kingdom"* (Heb. 1:8). In God's eternal Kingdom, one of the highest priorities is bringing Heaven's justice to earth, releasing heavenly solutions to solve the world's problems. This is our job as giant slayers. Like David, our hearts are meant to burn for God's justice. Like the Hebrews 11 heroes of faith, we are destined to administer God's justice on the earth (see Heb. 11:33-34).

As we discussed in chapter 2, we can know what cause or causes we are called to by the burning we feel in our hearts at the sight of an injustice. In this context, an *injustice* is anything that falls short of God's divine will. So, for example, if our hearts burn when we hear stories of people starving, that is our cause. If our hearts burn when we imagine movies that bring glory to God, that is our cause. If our hearts burn when we hear about another divorce, that is our cause. For me, my heart burns for those who have never heard the gospel once when some have heard it twice. The least, last, and the lost are my cause.

That burning in our hearts is Heaven's justice, readying itself to flow through us. David's heart burned with indignation at Goliath's insults, and that burning was the start of a plan to end that injustice. In the same way, when our hearts burn for a cause, that burning is a sign that God's divine solutions for those issues are available to us. When our hearts burn for His justice, the words in our mouths are anointed to bring freedom. And our hearts are filled with the courage needed to overcome the giants that stand in our way. God has given us His eyes to see His solutions for certain areas of life and parts of society. He has revealed to us the parts of His will that have not made it to earth yet, and He is ready to partner with us to see His justice made manifest. All we need to do is cultivate strong hearts that burn for the things of God.

An Unbreakable Heart

The third trait of those who do not lose heart is being unbreakable or unyielding. Often, slaying a giant is about having a heart that simply refuses to quit. Paul describes this quality by highlighting how not losing heart prepares us to receive breakthroughs that far outweigh the struggle:

> *Therefore we do not lose heart. Though outwardly we are wasting away, yet inwardly we are being renewed day by day. For our light and momentary troubles are achieving for us an eternal glory that far outweighs them all. So we fix our eyes not on what is seen, but on what is unseen, since what is seen is temporary, but what is unseen is eternal.*
>
> —2 CORINTHIANS 4:16-18

I experienced this in my own life during a season that some would refer to as the dark night of the soul. After experiencing great breakthrough where heaven invaded earth similar to that of Elijah in First Kings 18, I too experienced a rapid shift in my circumstances. Through boldness and courage, Elijah confronted all the false prophets of Baal, yet his battle was followed by a winter season. I refer to it as the battle you fight after the battle you have won. It is as if the spiritual climate has shifted from one season to another where you feel isolated, alone, and almost like you are molting. This gives deeper meaning to Isaiah's promise in Isaiah 40:31: *"Those who hope in the Lord will renew their strength. They will soar on wings like eagles; they will run and not grow weary, they will walk and not be faint."* Oftentimes we must persevere through hope in God's promises in order to overcome the giants we face. If our hearts are unwilling to give up, we cannot be defeated.

In the wake of two devastating back and neck injuries (the first I mentioned in chapter 1; the second I'll explain in chapter 7), I spent nine years on increasingly stronger pain medication. I had regained much of my mobility, and years of pain management therapy had made it possible for me to cope with my discomfort, but it was always there in varying degrees. Driven as I was, I had no plans to let pain (or anything else) stop me from doing the mission God had sent me here to do. I filled my schedule with ministry and travel, trying to make the most of the opportunities God gave me. I saw a lot of fruit during those years. People were healed, saved, and delivered. Amazing things happened. But there was a pain growing inside me, and it went beyond my physical discomfort.

Then, in 2003, tired and at the end of my rope, I began abusing the medication. My drug abuse went on for two years. My life felt like a swirl of drug-induced haziness, fluctuating pain, and a deep, aching fear clawing at the inside of my chest. I felt lost, alone, and ashamed. Finally, when it became clear that I needed help, on December 2, 2005 I checked into a treatment facility for twenty-eight days.

My entrance into the facility marked the beginning of one of the most trying times of my life. As soon as I entered I felt the presence of the Holy Spirit leave me. Lying there, feeling the pain of withdrawal compounded by the usual pain that came from my injuries, I slipped into utter despair. I called out to God and heard nothing. Without His nearness, I didn't know how to function. This seeming cold shoulder from God was the biggest pain of all. I felt like He had left me and let me down.

Those days in the treatment center, when I was unaware of God's presence and overwhelmed by hopelessness, were the longest days in my life. I couldn't see any hope. If someone had asked me, "Can you remember a single good thing God has done in your life?" I would have said *no*. I couldn't think about any of it. All I could see were dark clouds everywhere. During the twenty-eight days of treatment, I felt as though I was in the wilderness or the winter season where I was isolated and alone. In the spirit, I had lost the ability to soar, to see, and to think.

The second part of this season happened when I left the treatment center. For the next four months I remained at home, mostly confined to my bed, still unable to feel God's presence. I began crying out to God, but I still could not hear Him or see Him. It seemed as though He was playing hide-and-seek, and His hiding spot was way too hard. All I felt was hopelessness and despair. Day after day, I woke up and lived through another day of trying to press in to His presence—but all I got was exhaustion.

During this five-month season, first in the treatment center and then at home, although I was in the most difficult place I'd ever been, I refused to give up or lose heart. This was harder than the physical injuries I'd experienced, the addiction to medication, and various experiences of hurt and betrayal through the years. This was the hardest season in my life, in part because during it I lost both my dream and my vision. I couldn't look forward with hope, but still, I never gave up. I knew that after the sun sets it rises again in the morning. After the winter season comes the new life of spring. After the molting, the eagle gets new feathers. Or, as David put it, *"Weeping may stay for the night, but rejoicing comes in the morning"* (Ps. 30:5).

Refusing to lose heart in this season was very difficult. All I could do was live one day at a time, choosing to trust that God's words over my life would be fulfilled. Every day, I had to choose to get up one more time. I knew, if I could just get up one more time, I could make it. And one of those days, when I got up, I realized I was not just getting up to survive but to soar again. My season had shifted; I now was waiting for the winds of the Spirit to take me to higher places than ever before. After that long dark night of the soul, His presence had returned like a dove landing on my shoulder.

If we are brave enough, all it takes to overcome is to simply continue to get up and keep going as many times as we are knocked down. If we strengthen our hearts to never give up and to keep holding on, eventually we will get our breakthrough. Even in our moments of greatest and darkest despair, we cannot afford to lose heart. We may not always succeed. We may not always live up to our fullest potential, but God has put something special in each and every one of our hearts. If we learn to cultivate, protect, and mature our hearts, then there is truly no giant that can stand in our way. We will win if we don't lose heart.

STRENGTH TRAINING FOR OUR HEARTS

In his day, David was an extraordinary man, in large part because of the quality of his heart. While watching the sheep for his father, he had allowed God to shape him into a man after His own heart (see Acts 13:22), and as a result he stepped up when others ran away. In many ways, David was a man outside of his time because he experienced a level of intimacy with God that was uncommon under the old covenant. He experienced a taste of what is now readily available to all of us in the new covenant. Now, because of Jesus' death and resurrection, we are all capable of having hearts like David because Christ dwells in our hearts (see Eph. 3:17) and the unfathomable peace of God is the guard of our hearts (see Phil. 4:7; Col. 3:15).

Through the Holy Spirit, we receive an inner strength—the strength of faith—that surpasses our human resolve. Because of this, Jesus could say to His followers:

> *Truly I tell you, if anyone says to this mountain, "Go, throw yourself into the sea," and does not doubt in their heart but believes that what they say will happen, it will be done for them.*
> —MARK 11:23

This is the power of believing in our hearts. This is the power of those who refuse to lose heart. As giant slayers, we must learn to grow our hearts to be indestructible. We have to let the transforming presence of God strengthen our hearts so they cannot be broken, even when we are faced with the impossible.

David already had the heart of a giant slayer when Samuel showed up with the anointing oil. His father and brothers hadn't recognized it yet, but God had. The question is, how did David get his great shining heart? How did he cultivate the heart of a giant slayer? The answer is found in two constants in David's life—he took care of what God gave him, and he kept his eyes on God.

Be Diligent

As we talked about in chapter 1, much of David's ability to succeed as a giant slayer was due to his faithfulness in the small things. He didn't start being diligent when the big moment came. He spent his life practicing diligence. He stewarded what God gave him as though it was the most valuable task in the world. He did as Paul counseled the early believers, *"Whatever you do, work at it with all your heart, as working for the Lord"* (Col. 3:23). He gave his best effort while watching his father's sheep, day after day, for years. In this, he embodied Jesus' statement about how diligence in little things prepares us to be successful in big things: *"He who is faithful in a very little thing is faithful also in much; and he who is unrighteous in a very little thing is unrighteous also in much"* (Luke 16:10 NASB).

By taking good care of what was right in front of him, David developed the heart of a giant slayer and king. In the same way, if we wish to overcome the giants in our world we need to start by overcoming the little giants in our daily lives. Many people are passionate about overcoming the various giants at work in society, but they fail to see that the ability to overcome starts with being diligent and consistent in our own lives. Before we can mediate conflict between nations, we need to learn to have peaceful relationships with our family members. Before we can confront systemic poverty, we need to cultivate compassion for the unlovable and needy people in our workplace.

The weapons we will use to defeat the big giants of the world are the same as those we use to gain victory in our daily lives. These weapons include the fruit of the Spirit and the manifestation of godly character in our lives. Before we can dispense them to the world, we must learn how to use the weapons of joy, peace, and love in our families, at our workplaces, and at our local churches. We must learn to live the gospel on a small scale; this is the training needed to make our hearts mature enough to face the big giants and win. Every little challenge in life is an opportunity for growth. If we listen to the Holy Spirit when the little challenges come up, He will train us to recognize His voice when the big challenges arrive. If we let Him, God will make every day of our lives the training ground for our destiny. This is the power of diligence.

Look to Jesus

Not only did David cultivate diligence, but he also kept his focus on God. This is the second and most important key to cultivating a strong heart. Not surprisingly, it is also a major theme in the psalms David wrote. In Psalm 16, David said that keeping his eyes on the Lord enabled him to have an unshakable heart:

> *I will praise the Lord, who counsels me; even at night my heart instructs me. I keep my eyes always on the Lord. With him at my right hand, I will not be shaken. Therefore my heart is glad and my tongue rejoices; my body also will rest secure.*
>
> —PSALM 16:7-9

In Psalm 21, David said it was his trust in God that made him unshakable: *"For the king trusts in the Lord; through the unfailing love of the Most High he will not be shaken"* (Ps. 21:7). David learned how to turn to God, regardless of what was happening around him, for his strength and hope. Because he relied fully on God, the giants he faced could not cause him to lose heart. In Psalm 62, it is David's belief in God's strength and salvation that makes his heart strong: *"Truly he is my rock and my salvation; he is my fortress, I will never be shaken"* (Ps. 62:2, see also verse 6). Here, David refers to God as his fortress or stronghold.

In the Old Testament, a stronghold was a place of safety and refuge. Often, a stronghold was built on higher ground to give added protection and advantage over the enemy. In ancient warfare, the army that possessed the higher ground always had the advantage. This same principle applies to our spiritual lives. By fixing our eyes on Jesus, we cause our hearts to occupy the higher ground of the presence of God. In this way, we create a stronghold, or fortress, for ourselves against the enemy.

In the same way, when our eyes are on Jesus, our hearts will not be swayed or intimidated by the giants we face. In all circumstances, Paul's advice holds true: *"Since, then, you have been raised with Christ, set your hearts on things above, where Christ is, seated at the right hand of God"* (Col. 3:1). When we set our hearts on Christ and His heavenly truths, the difficulties of earth will not be able to overcome us. Keeping our eyes on Him enables us to see life the way He sees it. As a result, we will have the strength of heart to respond in faith. We will have the strength of heart to live like David did.

This is what it looks like to be imitators of Christ. He is our ultimate example of the unflinching heart of a giant slayer. Through His perseverance and strength of heart, He faced the greatest giant of all and overcame:

> *Let us run with perseverance the race marked out for us, fixing our eyes on Jesus, the pioneer and perfecter of faith. For the joy set before him he endured the cross, scorning its shame, and sat down at the right hand of the throne of God. Consider him who endured such opposition from sinners, so that you will not grow weary and lose heart.*
> —HEBREWS 12:1-3

His example and the grace He imparts in our lives can chase away weariness and keep us from losing heart. When we fix our eyes on Him, we become more and more like Him. And we learn to live like He lived and have a heart like His. We learn to be unshakable.

QUESTIONS TO PONDER

1. Have you ever experienced a season when all hope and vision for the future seemed lost? Did you find the strength you needed to keep moving forward and not give up? What is the best source of strength in times like this?

_____

_____

_____

_____

_____

_____

_____

_____

_____

2. In what areas of your life is God inviting you to live with greater diligence?

_____

_____

_____

_____

_____

_____

_____

_____

_____

3. David's heart immediately gave him a cause when he heard the mockery of Goliath. His heart burned. What areas of life and society make your heart burn? In what areas of your life can you cultivate greater faithfulness in small things so that you will be prepared to fight for the causes that burn in your heart?

_____

_____

_____

_____

_____

_____

_____

_____

_____

_____

DECLARATION

Through Christ, I have a strong and unflinching heart. I declare that no giant can cause me to lose heart because my eyes are fixed on Jesus, and He is my strength and security. No matter what is happening around me, I know my destiny in Him is secure. I know I will win simply because I will not give up.

RULE 6

IGNORE CRITICS AND FACE FEAR

When Eliab, David's oldest brother, heard him speaking with
the men, he burned with anger at him and asked, "Why have
you come down here? And with whom did you leave those few
sheep in the wilderness? I know how conceited you are and how
wicked your heart is; you came down only to watch the battle."
"Now what have I done?" said David. "Can't I even speak?"

—1 SAMUEL 17:28-29

Not everyone was excited to see David at the battlefield or to hear him ask questions about fighting the giant. David's oldest brother, Eliab, became angry at David and accused him of having wrong motives. Eliab assumed his little brother was shirking his duties at home and had sneaked away to see the action. So, he took it upon himself to reprimand him harshly and put him in his place, telling David that he was only a shepherd boy, and a wicked and conceited one at that. Clearly, Eliab was harboring some offense in his heart toward David.

Though we don't know much of the history between these two brothers, the likely cause for the tension between them and Eliab's aggressive and angry behavior can be found in the story of the prophet Samuel's anointing of the future king of Israel. As mentioned in the last chapter, not long before this battle, the prophet Samuel had visited the house of Jesse and anointed David—instead of Eliab—as the future king of Israel. This must have been quite the blow to Eliab's ego. In that day, being the eldest male child was a position of great significance. It came with responsibility and authority within the family. This would have been a huge part of Eliab's personal identity. Yet, when Samuel came, God passed over Eliab in favor of David.

Eliab may have outwardly seemed like an excellent choice, but according to God he did not measure up (see 1 Sam. 16:6-7). This reality would have been difficult for Eliab to accept. It was socially insulting for David to receive a higher honor than his eldest brother. Usually, this sort of transfer of honor only occurred when an elder sibling died or committed an act of great dishonor. Neither of those things had happened, yet inexplicably Samuel had chosen David over all of his older brothers. It is no surprise, then, that Eliab responded spitefully to David. Most likely, he was experiencing a great deal of insecurity and jealousy.

Not only did David receive harsh criticism from his brother, but he also received negative and critical feedback from King Saul. When David presented his idea to the king, Saul replied, *"You are not able to go out against this Philistine and fight him; you are only a young man, and he has been a warrior from his youth"* (1 Sam. 17:33). Imagine the conviction David must have felt to rebuff this criticism and negative feedback from the king. This was not just his older brother, but the king of Israel. Yet David felt so confident in God's calling that even the king's criticism seems to have had little impact on him. For David, showing up to face

Goliath involved ignoring the criticism and questioning of his brothers and King Saul and refusing to give in to the fears that often accompany criticism from others.

To face the giants in our lives, we too will need to ignore the critics. Success brings the fears and doubts of insecure people to light. The anointing always stirs up criticism. This was true of Eliab and doubly true of Saul. Later, David's success caused such fear and jealousy in Saul that Saul tried to kill David because he saw him as a threat to his throne. For this reason, when we show up to fight giants in our lives, we need to be prepared for criticism from others.

This criticism can manifest as harsh words and dissension disguised as input or correction. It can look like questioning our character or our ability to succeed. Regardless, criticism serves one purpose—to introduce fear into the situation in an attempt to sabotage a person's success. Insecure people don't like to see others succeed, because it challenges their lifestyle. Another person's success creates a contrast to their own experience and perhaps lesser degree of success. It may make them feel inadequate or cause them to question their own worth. As a result, like Eliab and Saul, they become critical and attack the potential for success in others.

Of course, critical people don't see it that way. They often don't realize what's going on in their hearts or why they feel the need to pull others down. Critics often think they are helping. I am sure Eliab felt justified in chastising David for leaving his duty with the sheep. I am sure Saul felt he was only being reasonable in telling David that he was sure to fail. Critics always seem to find a grain of truth to rub in our noses. They like to counter faith with logic. This is one reason why it is so important to be confident of our assignment. It helps us set our priorities.

It also helps us recognize the difference between constructive and destructive criticism. Much of the difference is in the way the feedback is delivered. Destructive criticism attacks the person and the vision. Eliab directly attacked David's character and motives. He wanted to put David in his place. Similarly, Saul criticized David's vision, saying it was impossible for him to succeed. These are the sorts of critics we should not listen to because they speak with the voice of the accuser. By contrast, constructive criticism (which we all need at times), affirms the person and the vision while offering feedback on how to make changes that will improve one's chance of success. Destructive criticism is designed to pull a person down, while constructive criticism is designed to raise a person up. Later in his life, David received constructive criticism, and he humbly listened to it (see 2 Sam. 12).

In this instance, the criticism he received was all designed to keep him from his destiny as a giant killer. His response to these critics is an example to us. David was focused on his assignment. He knew that something had to be done about the giant who was tormenting his people and insulting God's name. The time he had spent with the Lord had built enough faith to make him confident in engaging this task. Because of this, he did not allow his brother's words to offend or intimidate him. He just shrugged them off. He also did not argue with his brother. He responded in an honorable and straightforward manner and then continued on his way. When Saul also questioned his ability to succeed, David did not let Saul's fears become his own. Instead, he built his faith by testifying of God's goodness, something we'll talk more about in the next chapter. How we respond to criticism is just as important as whether or not we listen to criticism.

LIVING ABOVE THE VOICE OF CRITICISM

Years ago, I faced a great deal of criticism for a choice I made, but in the years since I have seen how staying true to what I believed God was telling me has born incredible fruit. One morning quite early, while at my Baptist church in Sandnes, Norway, I heard a knocking at the door. I'd been sitting in my office preparing a message on love. I walked to the door and looked through the glass to see a father, mother, and three small children. I could tell they were not from Norway. Feeling surprised and curious, I opened the door. With the few words of Norwegian they seemed to know, they begged me to allow them to come in. They were from Kosovo, a Muslim family seeking refuge in Norway because of the war. In their homeland, they faced mass persecution by the Serbs, so like many other families they had fled for their lives to Norway and were seeking shelter and protection.

The father told me they had just received a notice from the Norwegian government telling them they needed to return to Kosovo. They were desperate and willing to try anything to escape being sent back. So, they showed up at my church, praying someone would help them. After hearing their story, I felt I must try to help. We ended up hosting this family in our church building for several months, and during that time many people criticized me for trying to help them. Newspapers published articles criticizing me and our church. The police even threatened us. Many, many people questioned us, asking things like, "How could you break the law to help these people? How could you violate the church by letting Muslims live there?" The criticism came from many sources and lasted many years, even after this family had left.

I had no idea my actions would cause such an uproar. I also didn't know what fruit they would bear. But in the end, because we hosted this family they were able to remain in Norway and still live there to this day. What I did for them saved their lives. It also, these years later, has become the foundation for the open door that I have in the Muslim world. Of course, I had no idea of that back then. I was simply helping a family in need by showing them the practical love of Jesus. That practical demonstration of love is what Muslims need to see. My testimony of love in action, even in the face of criticism, speaks to their heart powerfully.

Not long ago, I was at an Islamic university where someone lectured me harshly because I am a Christian, saying, "How dare you talk about love!" In response, I was able to share with him my testimony of helping this Muslim family twenty years ago. Over and over, this story has broken down walls and shown Muslims what authentic love looks like. Not only that, but through advocating for this family despite the criticism, I learned how to be intentional and purposeful in my love for Muslims. It was my first experience in the school of criticism, and I am still experiencing the fruit of that season. Truly, when we do not let criticism shake us, it has the ability to make our resolve stronger and our love deeper. The ability to drown out the critics is one of the most significant differences between those who succeed in life and those who do not.

Every leader, great and small, faces a constant barrage of criticism. Hours of radio broadcasts, comedy sketches, and news analysis are devoted to criticizing every decision every president has ever made. Every pastor faces criticism, some spoken face to face and some spoken just out of earshot. Every leader in the Bible also faced tremendous criticism. Moses regularly faced the murmured criticism of the people he led to freedom. Noah's entire village thought he had gone crazy when he built the ark. Jesus was constantly attacked and criticized by the Pharisees. Even His disciples regularly questioned His methods. The point is, criticism is a normal part of facing the giants of life. It is the enemy's attack against the potential of success.

Critics will speak their dissension before, after, and during our seasons of success. They will say we don't deserve this, we're not good enough, we're not smart enough, we're wasting our time, and we only got lucky. As we travel down the path toward becoming giant slayers, we must cultivate selective hearing, like David did. We must listen to the voices that bring strength and encouragement and give helpful feedback while learning to ignore the voices that partner with fear.

FACING OUR FEAR

More often than not, people who are critical are people who have succumbed to fear at some point in their lives. Maybe they experienced a disappointment that caused them to become cynical as a form of self-protection. Maybe they submitted to fear and ran away from their giants. Whatever the reason, most people with a critical spirit are operating from a place of fear. As giant slayers, it is our job to learn how to have victory over fear in our own lives and then teach others how to have the same victory.

Fear is the first attack of a giant. Fear seeks to paralyze us and prevent us from ever actually engaging the battle with our giant. This is one of the primary purposes of the voice of criticism—to introduce fear. I'm sure David felt flickers of fear as he faced criticism from Eliab and Saul. Then, when he walked down into the valley to face his giant, those fears must have been shouting in his head. After all, Saul's army had been paralyzed by the fear of Goliath. He was no small opponent. Yet David simply decided to push past that fear and do what God was telling him to do. This is the definition of true courage—*faith demonstrated in radical action in the presence of fear.* David did not let the fear, or the criticism that was designed to confirm that fear, determine his actions.

We must respond courageously, like David did. When we feel fear, we must choose to face it instead of giving it a place in our hearts. This is crucial because fear is first *perceived* and then *received.* It often starts as a perception or mindset. However, if we entertain it, it can progress in the spiritual realm. Then, the lies of the enemy become a stronghold in our minds. A stronghold is a safe place in our lives for demonic spirits. Certain mindsets, like fear, predispose us to demonic influence. For this reason, we must immediately squash them and step into faith in God's truth. If we do not, we open ourselves to the vicious cycle of fear. It paralyzes us and prevents us from acting. This inaction leads to a lack of experience.

Without experience, we cannot escape our ignorance about the things we fear. When we do not understand something, our ignorance breeds fear, and thus the cycle begins anew.

Without doubt, the greatest hindrance to our ability to step into our divine destiny is fear. Fear, which is rooted in unbelief, holds us back from the purposes of God. Unbelief thrives in a heart that is not in alignment with God's nature, purpose, power, and presence. Because of this, every giant slayer must confront unbelief and come face to face with fear. There is no way around it. To step into freedom, we need to deal with unbelief and fear—first within us and then around us.

Thankfully, our heavenly Father has given us everything we need to defeat fear. As the apostle Paul said, *"God has not given us a spirit of fear, but of power and of love and of a sound mind"* (2 Tim. 1:7 NKJV). These three gifts from God—power, love, and a sound mind—are the keys to saying *no* to fear in our lives. God has given us *power* to overcome the circumstances of life, *love* to overcome the fear of others, and *a sound mind* to overcome our weaknesses and live with self-control. These are not abstract principles but tools that God has placed in our hands to help us overcome every lie that fear throws in our direction. All we need is to know how to use them.

1. Power—To Face Our Circumstances

The first key to overcoming fear is learning to walk in the power of God. When we face overwhelming circumstances, we can respond to them in one of three ways—we can run from them, we can ignore them, or we can face them. The first two options are rooted in fear. The third option, facing our circumstances, is the choice to step into God's gift of power in our lives. God has given us the power to overcome. This is a gift we have received as part of our inheritance in Christ. God has designed us to be powerful. God's power in our lives is His divine ability, which enables us to do the impossible.

We are powerful because of His power mightily working within us (see Eph. 3:20). When we receive new life in Him, we become overcomers. It is part of our new nature as sons and daughters of the Almighty God. Because of this, we can say with Paul, *"I can do all things through Christ who strengthens me"* (Phil. 4:13 NKJV). Only in Him and by His power can we overcome. But when we are walking in His power, nothing can stand in the way of our destiny. This power is part of our inheritance as God's children, yet we need to allow the Holy Spirit to work through us to access the power that is already available. Jesus told His disciples, *"You will receive power when the Holy Spirit comes on you"* (Acts 1:8). Through the Holy Spirit at work in our lives, we have the power we need to face fear and confront the overwhelming circumstances of our lives. It really is this simple. Yet, many of us do not believe it.

Because facing our fears is the only way we can overcome them, it is essential to know that we are capable of facing our fears. This may seem obvious, but it is the foundation of overcoming fear. There is no point in trying to face our fears if we do not believe we have been given the power to overcome our circumstances. I could write page after page outlining how much power and authority God has bestowed upon us by sending His Son Jesus to die on our behalf. I cannot impart with words what can only be understood by revelation. God says He has given us a spirit of power. The only way we can become familiar with the heights and depths of this promise is to begin facing our fears. The Holy Spirit has come as our teacher and comforter, but if we run or hide from our fears, we also run and hide from the solutions the Holy Spirit is ready to give us.

This is the cycle of fear, as mentioned above. If we never risk facing our fears, then we will never experience what it feels like for the Holy Spirit to guide us through our fears. Without an experience, the promise that we have been given a spirit of power will feel like empty words. We need to jump off the cycle of fear and jump into the cycle of faith. We do this by choosing to take a risk and trust in God's promise of power to overcome, even when we don't have an experience to authenticate that promise. That is true faith—believing before we see. To engage faith, we must face the fears that have held us back. The Holy Spirit will then guide us from victory to victory to victory. The more experience in facing and overcoming our fears we get, the more trust we will have in God's promises and power. Facing our fears creates an opportunity for us to learn the goodness of God by experience and revelation, not just by words.

2. Love—To Face Others

The second key to overcoming fear is love. According to the Bible, love is the antidote to fear. *"There is no fear in love. But perfect love drives out fear, because fear has to do with punishment. The one who fears is not made perfect in love"* (1 John 4:18). Love deals with the roots of fear. It disarms and dissipates it. This is true, first, in our relationship with God and, second, in our relationships with others. First, we allow God's love to chase out the fear in our hearts—the fear that He will let us down or punish us when we fail, as well as the fear that others will hurt us. Second, through our experience of God's love, we learn to fearlessly love others.

It's hard to fear someone we share mutual love with because love creates a bond of protection and mutual value. It also equips us to hear what the Holy Spirit is saying about the people around us. People don't seem like obstacles when our relationships are built on the foundation of love. Instead, as we learn to give and receive love, we create a healthy flow that washes the fear from our lives. A lifestyle of loving and being loved empowers us to stand up to fear. We all need healthy spiritual fathers and mothers pouring into our lives, strong peers running beside us, and spiritual sons and daughters whom we are pouring into. This fosters a flow of love and encouragement that causes healthy growth in us and in the people around us. And it gives us the strength we need to face and overcome our fears.

3. A Sound Mind—To Face Ourselves

The third key to overcoming fear is cultivating a sound mind. *A sound mind* can be defined as "wisdom and understanding that leads to Kingdom lifestyle choices, habits, and mindsets." In other words, a sound mind is a mind that thinks according to Heaven's perspective. The Bible promises that we have been given a sound mind, or the mind of Christ (see 1 Cor. 2:16). Just as God has given us power and love as part of our inheritance in Christ, He has also given us a sound mind. Yet it is our responsibility to posture ourselves to live in the reality of what He has already given us. Paul put it this way:

> *Since, then, you have been raised with Christ, set your hearts on things above, where Christ is, seated at the right hand of God. Set your minds on things above, not on earthly things. For you died, and your life is now hidden with Christ in God.*
> —COLOSSIANS 3:1-3

This is crucial, because half of the battle is won in the mind. Our own minds can be our greatest source of fear. I still remember sitting in the doctor's office as a small boy, writhing in frightful anticipation at the thought of a tiny needle being stuck into my arm. After an hour of fretting and sweating, I clenched my teeth as the nurse approached with the syringe in hand. Then, the quick pinch of the needle was there and gone faster than I could blink. The suffering brought on by the fear of the needle was so much greater than the actual pain it caused. Nearly all fear is like this. We build up our problems in our minds, stretching and expanding them until they are impassible mountains, when in reality they are only gently rolling hills.

The apostle Paul gives us insight with two important statements in Romans 12:2—*"And do not be conformed to this world, but be transformed by the renewing of your mind, that you may prove what is that good and acceptable and perfect will of God"* (NKJV). First, he exhorts

119

us to not be conformed to this world. We cannot let what is normal and possible in this world become the standard that we set for the Kingdom of God. Our Lord's ways are too perfect for that. We cannot afford to let the circumstances of our past, the failures of others, or the scenarios we build in our minds determine how much of God's power and authority we allow in our lives. To prevent this from happening, we must follow Paul's second statement and be transformed by the renewing of our minds.

The transformation and renewal of the mind doesn't happen overnight or by accident. When salvation occurs, we receive the mind of Christ. It is fully ours, yet we must learn to take possession of what we have received. Little by little, day by day, as we do the things that bring glory to Him, we will experience transformation in our minds. Paul said it best in Philippians 4:8—*"Finally, brothers and sisters, whatever is true, whatever is noble, whatever is right, whatever is pure, whatever is lovely, whatever is admirable—if anything is excellent or praiseworthy—think about such things."* We cultivate a sound mind by meditating on the things of God.

Starting the process of overcoming fear is simple. We need only to look our fears in the eye and ask the Holy Spirit to show us how to overcome them. He may immediately give us strategies to overcome fear in that very moment, or He may have us begin with baby steps. He is the perfect teacher. He knows just what we need to make all fear come to an end in our lives. All we need to do is face our fears. We can do this, boldly and bravely, because the Bible assures us that love is indeed stronger than fear.

LOVE IS STRONGER

Fear does not need to win in our lives because the perfect love of God casts out fear. This is one of the most reassuring promises of the

Bible, and it should provoke us to take action against fear in our lives. We should not be content to let fear stay or to give it control over parts of our lives. Many people have accepted fear as a normal part of life. They feel more comfortable coordinating their lives to work around their fears than directly facing them and overcoming them. It can be hard to motivate ourselves to face the fears in our lives, especially if we have spent the majority of our lives making room for those fears. But, it is important to remember that no matter how long fear has had control of our lives, love is always stronger than fear. If we shine the light of God's love and allow His love to embolden us, those fears cannot keep their grip on our hearts.

For many years, I allowed a childhood experience to create a place for fear in my life. When I was quite young, I was attacked by a dog. When I reached out my hand to pet the dog, it lunged forward and bit me on the hand. I still have the scar. From that moment on, I had a very strong fear of dogs. This fear seemed to attract them to me. If I visited someone who had a dog, it would immediately run up to me, even if several other people had entered the room at the same time. This was difficult for me, and at times it caused me to avoid people or situations because I knew a dog would be present. This was something I struggled with for most of my life.

Then, one day the Holy Spirit spoke to me about my fear of dogs. I saw a picture in my mind's eye of a dog moving to attack a cat. As I saw the scene play out, I heard the Holy Spirit ask, "Leif, would you save that cat?"

Though I felt badly about my answer, I knew had to be honest. "No," I said. "I would not save the cat. I am too scared of dogs."

Then the Holy Spirit showed me a picture of the same dog moving to attack my youngest daughter. Immediately, I felt a jolt of anger and strength leap up in my heart. I was ready to leap on that dog in half a second, without even a thought. As I felt this, I heard the Holy Spirit speak again, "You see, love is more powerful than fear."

Fear can seem like an unbeatable opponent. It is one of the giants that overwhelms and sidelines the most people. But fear doesn't have to win. Love is all it takes to overcome any amount of fear. The apostle John tells us clearly, "*There is no fear in love. But perfect love drives out fear, because fear has to do with punishment. The one who fears is not made perfect in love*" (1 John 4:18). When we are made perfect in love—when we receive a full revelation of God's love for us and all that His love entails—we are freed from the grip of fear. Love is a light that drives out the darkness of fear. God the Father, the author and embodiment of love, loves us everlastingly. He wants to overwhelm us with His love, which will cause us to fall so in love with Him and His people that we will not fear to face any giant that may stand in our way. God's perfect love is the power we need. It settles deep down in our hearts—telling us who we are and what we were born to do—and it gives us the confidence we need to ignore our critics and face our fears.

QUESTIONS TO PONDER

1. Why do you think David's courage drew so much criticism from his older brother and King Saul? Have you experienced this in your life? How did you respond?

_____

_____

_____

_____

_____

_____

_____

2. What's the difference between constructive criticism and destructive criticism? What fruit has each borne in your life?

_____

_____

_____

_____

_____

_____

3. The spirit of fear seeks to paralyze us and prevent us from attaining our God-given destiny in every area of our lives. Name some of the ways that fear has held you back in the following areas. Then spend a few minutes asking the Holy Spirit what His strategy is for you to overcome these fears.

   ▪ In your home and family:

_____

_____

_____

_____

_____

_____

_____

_____

- In your job:

_____

_____

_____

_____

_____

_____

- In your personal relationships:

_____

_____

_____

_____

_____

_____

DECLARATION

Today I declare that I am no longer a slave to fear. I will not listen to the destructive voice of criticism or believe the fear it seeks to impart. Instead, I believe what God says about me, and I choose to confidently obey His call. Because of God's love in my heart, I have power, love, and a sound mind to overcome all fear. From now on, I will not passively accept or allow fear a place in my life. Instead, I step into love because perfect love drives out fear. I am confident that whenever I encounter fear, the Holy Spirit will give me His strategies for overcoming that fear, and I will have the courage needed to face every giant.

RULE 7

CELEBRATE PAST VICTORIES

But David said to Saul, "Your servant has been keeping his father's sheep. When a lion or a bear came and carried off a sheep from the flock, I went after it, struck it and rescued the sheep from its mouth. When it turned on me, I seized it by its hair, struck it and killed it. Your servant has killed both the lion and the bear; this uncircumcised Philistine will be like one of them, because he has defied the armies of the living God. The Lord who rescued me from the paw of the lion and the paw of the bear will rescue me from the hand of this Philistine." Saul said to David, "Go, and the Lord be with you."

—1 SAMUEL 17:34–37

When David heard Goliath's threats and insults, a righteous indignation rose up in his chest. He knew he had to do something. His sense of call and his courage caused him to begin asking the men around him what the king would do for the man who fought Goliath. When the king got ear of David's questions, he summoned him to his tent. There, David confidently declared his intention to fight the giant. As we discussed in the last chapter, Saul was less than enthusiastic about David's idea. Essentially, he told him, "There's no way you can fight that giant and live." It's not surprising that Saul would doubt David's ability. Not only was he prone to fearing those who might outshine him, but Goliath was a formidable opponent.

David's confidence, especially when contrasted with the fear of the experienced Israeli army, must have seemed like laughable naïveté. Saul was an experienced warrior and a war hero in his own right. Yet even he was not lining up to fight Goliath. Saul and his men were not cowards. They were simply seasoned warriors who recognized the immensity of the challenge before them. They were, in some ways, wise to avoid conflict with the giant. It is no wonder, then, that Saul immediately discounted David. Nothing on the outside of David indicated that he would have even a chance of success.

Yet David did not let this discourage him. Instead, he responded to Saul's doubts by sharing a few of his personal experiences with God. David had seen God come through and help him overcome the odds, and he knew God would do it again. David had seen seemingly insurmountable situations before. He had faced terrifying opponents who seemed to have the advantage, and yet he had come out the victor. This was his experience, and because of it he believed God would help him overcome Goliath. In other words, David recited his history as a defense for the likelihood of his future success. This account of God's goodness swayed King Saul, and he gave David permission to fight the giant.

This change of heart has always fascinated me. Saul could have assumed David was lying about the bear and the lion. He could have labeled him a hotheaded boy looking for a fight and a bit of glory. Further, even if Saul believed David's story, killing two wild animals is not the same as fighting a well-trained and experienced soldier. Saul would have known this well, yet something about David's story swayed his heart. I believe this happened because of the power inherent in reminding ourselves of the victories of the past. Even if those victories are smaller than the problems we now face, it is easy to remember when those old problems felt impossibly big. Remembering the process of past victories gives us the courage to attempt the impossible again.

We all have victories in our history—moments when circumstances were dire, yet all the pieces came together at the last second. Some of these victories are small, and some are big. We all also have defeats in our history—times when we made poor choices or when the choices of others caused havoc in our lives. Too often, we remember what we should forget and forget what we should remember. We have a choice when viewing our own personal history. We can live with our failures as the standard, or we can live with our victories as the standard.

David chose to live with his eye on his past victories, and this gave him the grit he needed to believe he could win against Goliath. Later in his life, we see David making a similar choice when he was faced with the devastation of his city, the kidnapping of his family, and the rumblings of betrayal from his men. In the face of such dire circumstances, David strengthened himself in the Lord (see 1 Sam. 30:6). I believe one of the ways he did this was by recalling his history with God and the many times God had come through for him in the past. Based on that history, he strengthened his heart to have hope for the future.

Like few others in biblical history, David understood the value of remembering his history with God. The remembrance brought him to an encounter with God. In that encounter, he not only received encouragement but also a strategy for how to defeat the enemy and recover what had been stolen. The encounter was so powerful that it changed David *and* the people around him, who were about to stone him because of their grief. Supernaturally, when David remembered his past victories with God, courage and boldness came alive in the hearts of everyone.

In the same way, our history with God should serve as a powerful reminder of His nature and power in our lives. We access the grace and the anointing of our personal encounters with God in past seasons by *remembering* those encounters and our experiences of God's faithfulness. Often, the best way to recalibrate our thinking and perspective is to remind ourselves of our testimonies with God.

Knowing that God has come through for us in the past brings strength to our present. Many of us do not celebrate our past victories with God nearly enough. We can tell whether we need to increase our celebration by asking ourselves, *What is the first thing that fills my heart when a new giant shows up in my life—fear or faith, intimidation or celebration?* When our minds are being continually renewed by the testimony of past victories, our instinctual response to giants will be faith-filled and confident, just like David's. But if we are not careful to celebrate the past, we will become fearful and timid like Saul's army, afraid to fight Goliath. We must determine to never forget the testimony of God's great work in us. This is an important key to overcoming, as we see in the example of the saints of Revelation: *"And they overcame* [the accuser] *by the blood of the Lamb and by the word of their testimony"* (Rev. 12:11 NKJV). The same will be true for us! We simply need to learn to remember.

LEARNING TO REMEMBER

I learned the power of remembering in my personal struggle with pain after the accident in the pool (that I mentioned in chapter 1). It took me a long time to learn to live normally after the accident. Three years later, I finally decided to stop taking the pain medication I had been prescribed. The prospect was frightening. I still dealt with a great deal of pain and discomfort, but I did not want to become dependent on the medicine. So, I committed to going forty days without taking any pills.

On the thirty-ninth day of my fast, I was being driven from one event to another during a visit to Norway. We were a little late, and the driver was trying to hurry along the winding mountainous road. As we were going around a corner, the driver lost control of the car, and it slammed into the side of the mountain. A car behind us also slipped off the road and crashed into the back of us. My back, leg, and ribs were instantly broken. My injuries were so extensive I required six surgeries, and I spent nine months in what basically amounted to a full body cast and wheelchair.

I spent the first few weeks in an all too familiar cloud of pain and despair. *How could this happen again?* I wondered. Life had just started getting back to normal. I had continued to serve the Lord, even when my pain was overwhelming. I had been one day away from completing my commitment to staying off medication. Now, I was starting all over again, but with even worse injuries. I fought to stay in control of my thoughts. The feelings of frustration and sense of injustice were overwhelming. I was weak again. I was disabled again. I didn't know if I would get better. In the face of this, all my old fears returned. *Will I be able to hold my grandchildren? Will I be able to preach? Will I be able to walk without pain?*

In this new place of darkness, I felt the light of God's presence shine through once again. I remembered how His presence had sustained me through my last great trial, and deep down I knew He would do it again. I felt tempted to look at my new trial as evidence of God's lack of faithfulness. The reality was, God's faithfulness was the guarantee of my success. This renewed revelation did not bring immediate change to my physical pain or even my emotional distress; however, it did give me something to hold on to. It was both painful and humbling to start back at the beginning with a new disability, but it was a trial I had overcome in the past through the presence of the Holy Spirit, and I knew that, with Him, I could do it again.

This was the power of testimony at work in my life. The word *testimony* in the Bible is more literally translated as "do it again." Our testimonies are meant to be watermarks of the relationship and authority that we have because of our God. They are the standard by which we are meant to live. It would be dishonest for me to say that it was easy to hold on to my own testimony when this new disaster invaded my life, but it was the only thing that gave me the strength to press past the pain and into my Father's arms.

The enemy tries to use trials to separate us from God. He fills our ears with lies, telling us that God has abandoned us or that He doesn't care. Trials are meant to bring us closer to God. I do not believe God causes suffering in our lives. No good father would do that. Most pain comes from our own mistakes or the mistakes of those around us. However, God wants to use the opportunity that trials and tribulations present to pull us closer to Him. As our Father, He wants us to know He is with us every step of the way. He doesn't want us to merely survive the storms of life; He wants us to learn to navigate them victoriously. We do this by recalling our past victories and remembering who Jesus is for us. When these memories of His faithfulness are more real to us than the trials of our present, we will have the keys we need to face our giants with faith.

A LESSON TO NEVER FORGET

Of course, learning to trust God and to remember the victories of the past is something we are all growing in. It is a process we all need to walk out daily. Even Jesus' original disciples, who walked with Him for three years and saw many miracles, needed to learn to grow in trust for Him. One of the greatest stories of this happened when Jesus and His disciples were sailing across the sea and encountered a furious storm. It was not unusual for storms to blow up on the Sea of Galilee. It is in a basin surrounded by mountains and is notorious for furious storms. Rising just to the north, over the lake, is beautiful Mount Hermon. Mount Hermon is capped with snow, and sometimes the cold air from the top of Hermon rushes down the mountain and blows across the sea. The force of the cold air meeting the hot moist air around Galilee can be explosive, as it was on that day.

In the face of such a storm, the disciples panicked. Though several of them were experienced fishermen, they were convinced they were going to drown. Clearly, it was a bad storm. Yet somehow, even as the storm grew in size and intensity, Jesus was sleeping in the back of the boat.

Frustrated that He could be asleep while their lives were in danger, the disciples awoke Him with an accusation: *"Teacher, don't you care if we drown?"* (Mark 4:38). In this telling question, the core of their fear is revealed. They had forgotten who Jesus is. They had forgotten all the miracles, all the kindness, and all the things He had taught them. They had forgotten the victories of the past, and as a result they saw only the crisis of the present. In the face of a frightening storm, they had forgotten all of the experiences that had taught them who Jesus is. Because of this, they were acting like victims instead of overcomers.

In response to their panic, Jesus got up and rebuked the wind and waves. Immediately the storm died down, and the sea was completely calm. Then, He turned to His disciples and asked, *"Why are you so afraid? Do you still have no faith?"* (Mark 4:40).

This terrified them even more, and they said to one another, *"Who is this? Even the wind and the waves obey him!"* Mark 4:41).

The disciples had forgotten who Jesus really is, and as a result they responded to their situation in fear. For this reason, Jesus took the opportunity to, yet again, reveal His character. In His simple question, He reminded them of all they had forgotten. *"Do you still have no faith?"* Their faith in Jesus, based on what He had already done for them, should have given them the courage they needed to face that storm unafraid. It should have given them the boldness to do what Jesus then did for them—rebuke the wind and waves. Otherwise, Jesus would not have rebuked them for feeling afraid of the storm. Otherwise, He would not have purposefully slept in the boat, leaving His disciples to handle the storm alone. He knew they had what it took to overcome, but they panicked, and He came to their rescue. This is why He rebuked them so strongly. They were not acting like the giant slayers He knew they were.

In this story, we find several lessons about how Heaven approaches crisis and how to maintain our faith when we face giants. No matter what we face, if we remember these truths we will be equipped with a proper perspective, which will help us see our situations with God's eyes and respond like the giant slayers we are made to be.

1. The Storm Often Comes in the Path of Obedience

First, we must remember that it was Jesus' idea to cross the sea. *"He said to his disciples, 'Let us go over to the other side'"* (Mark 4:35). When Jesus said, "Let's go to the other side," He was not asking for an opinion. He was telling them what to do. Jesus was the one who came up with the idea, not the disciples. They were simply obeying Him, and on the path of obedience they encountered a storm they thought would kill them. Jesus, of course, being Jesus, must have known they would encounter a storm. Yet He told them to cross the sea anyway. From this we can learn that Jesus is not afraid of storms, and He doesn't think we should be either. He knows we are capable of passing through them. When we face a storm, it's always good to remember that He didn't deliver the disciples *from* the storm, but He took them *through* it. The same is often true for us.

I have heard many people say, "The safest place to be is in the center of God's will." That depends on our definition of the word *safe*. Safety is not avoiding the storm; safety is having a Father who will teach us how to weather any storm. He doesn't want us to hide from storms; He wants to teach us to navigate and command them. Risk is inherent to greatness. We cannot become giant slayers if we never face any giants. We cannot be atmosphere-shifters if we never stand up to any storms. This may seem intimidating, but it is what we are made for. And we have the promise that God will guide us through whatever may come against us and that we will progress from glory to glory (see Isa. 58:11; 2 Cor. 3:18). As Jesus told His disciples, *"These things I have spoken to you, that in Me you may have peace. In the world you will have tribulation; but be of good cheer, I have overcome the world"* (John 16:33 NKJV). We will face giants in this life, but we do not need to worry because He has overcome and we get to share in His victory.

2. *It May Feel Like Jesus Doesn't Care*

The second lesson the disciples learned was that when we face a storm, it may sometimes seem like Jesus doesn't care about our survival. The disciples felt so abandoned and betrayed by Jesus' decision to sleep in the storm that they accused Him of not caring if they drowned. Their desperation at its peak, the disciples turned to look for Jesus, only to find their last hope taking a nap in the back of the boat. It is not difficult to see how this might have made them feel. We have the greater context of the story to let us know that everything will turn out all right, but the disciples were sure they were going to die.

We have all experienced similar moments. We call out to God, overwhelmed by the circumstances of life or a sudden crisis, and He doesn't answer. Or, He doesn't answer in the way we expect. Instead of instantly fixing our problem, He may simply say, "I love you," or, "Rest in My peace." These are not the answers we want to hear. We want solutions, and now. But usually, that is not how Jesus works. It is easy to get frustrated or even offended in these moments. Peace is offensive when we are living in fear.

But, if we want to overcome, we need to notice what Jesus is doing in moments like these. The truth is, He is not abandoning us. Instead, Jesus points to the internal provision (things like peace and joy) that will help us overcome the external struggle. He shows us the tools He has given us that will help us to be victorious. Jesus wants us to learn to see the world through Heaven's eyes. Big problems look much smaller from Heaven. God's peace, when we are in crisis, may feel uncompassionate, but it is just the opposite. It is His invitation into a place of perfect, incomprehensible peace that knows the way through every storm (see Phil. 4:7).

Also, in moments like these, Jesus is choosing not to rescue us so that we can learn how to step into the power He's given us and enforce His victory. His desire for all of us is that we would grow up into mature sons and daughters (see Eph. 4:13–15). We are not designed to live as helpless and needy victims but as powerful and confident victors. To help us learn this, sometimes Jesus seems to leave us alone in crisis. He is like the mother eagle who pushes her baby from the nest to teach him to fly. That mother will not allow the baby to fall to the ground and die. She is keeping a watchful eye on him. Yet to the baby, it may seem like the mother has abandoned him. This may seem uncaring, but by choosing not to rescue the baby, the mother is empowering the baby to fly and learn to care for himself. Often, Jesus does not rescue us from our giants because He wants us to learn to fight them ourselves. He's already given us what we need to win, and He's proven Himself to us in the past. Now, as with the disciples, He wants us to be the ones who exercise His authority and calm the storm. Remembering this will help us avoid offense and face our giants with courage.

3. The Storm Drives Us to Jesus

The third lesson is that every storm can be turned to our benefit if we allow it to drive us closer to Jesus. Jesus asked His disciples two questions: *"Why are you afraid?"* and *"Have you no faith?"* He wanted to share the peace He had with them and empower them to fight their own battles, but first He had to adjust their perspective. They had responded in fear when they should have responded in faith. This made all the difference in their ability to cope with and overcome the storm.

Fear and faith, in some ways, are very much alike. They both believe in something they can't see. Fear believes something disastrous will happen. Faith believes something positive will happen. Fear will drive us to fix the problem any way we can. Faith will drive us to the one source who can do something about our problem—Jesus. Faith causes us to remember our past victories with Jesus, and it stirs us to believe for a similar outcome in our present. In fear, the disciples began accusing Jesus of abandoning them. Had they responded in faith, they would have had peace and assurance of God's protection, and they would have trusted Jesus to rescue them. Perhaps they would have even stepped into the authority Jesus had given them and commanded the storm to be still.

When we walk in faith, remembering the testimonies of God's goodness in our lives, storms will always bring us closer to Jesus. They will cause us to step into His peace and to ask Him for wisdom and strategy for the storm. Yes, at times the storms of life may seem overwhelming, but if they bring us into a place of deeper intimacy with God then they are well worth the trouble.

4. No Storm Can Wreck the Purpose of God

Fourth, from this story we can find the assurance that God's purposes are bigger than any storm. On the other side of the sea, where Jesus and the disciples were heading, waited a demon-possessed man who longed to be set free. Also, after passing through the storm they would meet a woman with a terrible disease, yearning to be healed, and a young girl who needed to be restored to life (see Mark 5). When we are in the middle of a storm, it can be hard to imagine anything good coming of it. The disciples had the same problem. However, what they failed to realize was that as long as Jesus was on board they were going to make it to the other side. The storm was no real threat to Jesus' destiny—or to the destiny of His disciples. Yet Jesus used it to teach His disciples an important lesson that would take them to the next level of anointing. He often does the same with us. It is one thing to have the *peace of God* in our hearts and quite another to have the *God of peace* leading our lives.

5. *We Must Remember Who Jesus Is*

The fifth and ultimate lesson of this story is the importance of remembering who Jesus is. The disciples had seen Jesus perform many amazing miracles before they took their trip through the storm. When we see breakthrough, when we see God at work in our lives, it creates a kind of responsibility. We are responsible to remember the works of God and live our lives expecting Him to continue being who He is. The disciples forgot, if only for a few moments, who Jesus is. Their fear was so great that they even questioned if Jesus cared at all.

We all have storms come up in our lives. Sometimes the defeated giants of yesterday suddenly rear their heads again today. Sometimes something that should have been simple spirals out of control and becomes overwhelming. Sometimes our circumstances become so dire that we can no longer find hope. It is in these moments that we must remember who Jesus is. We must remember yesterday's victories so that we have the courage to face today's giants.

Each of these five lessons from the story of Jesus calming the storm is rooted in the need for genuine faith in God, based not on what we can see but on what we know of Him from our personal history. He has not failed us in the past, and He will not fail us again. He has performed miracles in the past, and He will do so again. He is the same yesterday, today, and forever—our ever faithful Father and friend (see Heb. 13:8). This belief— and the discipline of recalling our past victories—is crucial to our ability to overcome the giants in our lives. The narrative we remind ourselves of, either of victory or defeat, will determine our response in the present. We must choose, like David did, to listen to the narrative of faith, the narrative of our victories.

QUESTIONS TO PONDER

1. When David was challenged by King Saul concerning his qualifications to take on Goliath, he recounted his past victories. List some of your own personal victories. How do these apply to any giants you are facing today?

2. The disciples saw Jesus asleep in the back of the boat. Do you think He was really asleep? Or do you think He was testing them to see how they would react to the storm?

3. Pick a situation that worries you. It can be big or small. Invite the Holy Spirit to release peace into that situation. Ask Him to remind you of relevant victories from your past. What did He tell you?

_____

_____

_____

_____

4. Explain the difference between faith and fear. What steps can you take to cultivate greater faith?

_____

_____

_____

_____

_____

_____

Declaration

When I face the giants of life, I declare that I will strengthen myself in God by remembering His faithfulness to me and my past victories. I will make victory, not failure, the standard for my life, and I will live with a faith-filled expectation for great outcomes and supernatural victories over the giants I face and the storms I walk through.

RULE 8

SEEK THE REWARD

Now the Israelites had been saying, "Do you see how this man keeps coming out? He comes out to defy Israel. The king will give great wealth to the man who kills him. He will also give him his daughter in marriage and will exempt his family from taxes in Israel." David asked the men standing near him, "What will be done for the man who kills this Philistine and removes this disgrace from Israel? Who is this uncircumcised Philistine that he should defy the armies of the living God?"

—1 SAMUEL 17:25-26

When David heard Goliath threatening the army of Israel, the first question he asked was, "What will I get for fighting this giant?" He knew a victory that big would come with a large reward. Some have criticized David for asking about the reward. They have suggested that this question is evidence of David's humanity and a touch of greed. In fact, it is exactly the opposite. David saw, in the opportunity to fight Goliath, what so many of us miss. He saw the road to his destiny. This road involved some very specific material rewards that, under natural circumstances, were out of David's reach. Now, suddenly, this crisis had given David an unexpected opportunity to gain three specific rewards that were key to his destiny as future king of Israel. Not only could he rid the land of this offense against God's name, but by doing so he could earn rewards that would propel him toward his destiny.

This principle is also true in our lives. The biggest giants produce the greatest rewards. As giant slayers, it is our destiny to face off with giants. We destroy them for the sake of God's glory and to further His Kingdom. But, these giants are not merely obstacles and hindrances. They are also gateways to great promotion and reward. In fact, giants are not in the way of our destiny; they are a part of it. Whatever is sent to destroy us will actually become a footstool to promote us.

David recognized this, and he received a lot for his victory. He gained favor with the king, finances for his family, and relationship with the king through marrying his daughter. This was the first step on his journey toward becoming king. In the same way, our victories over giants will bring wealth, both physical and spiritual, into our lives. We do not fight giants for the wealth and promotion, but they are benefits that come to us because of our faithfulness, and they are tools that help us further God's purposes. We use the wealth and influence gained from our victories to bring blessing and freedom to others. In this way, the giants or enemies we face are actually a key part of our journey to the destiny that God has for us.

THE BENEFITS OF ENEMIES

We all have enemies. Our lives are part of a spiritual conflict between God and the forces of evil. As God's children and ambassadors of His Kingdom on earth, it is only natural that we will encounter enemies who seek to overcome us. These enemies typically take two forms—people who directly oppose us and circumstances that could distract or derail us from our destiny. The root of both of these enemies is the same—the spiritual forces of wickedness. In other words, people and situations are not our true enemies. Though they may oppose us, they are puppets in the hands of our true enemy, Satan.

This is important to remember, especially as we interact with people who oppose us. God's heart is always for people, and He wants all people to be saved (see 1 Tim. 2:4). For this reason, we must follow Jesus' command—*"Love your enemies and pray for those who persecute you"* (Matt. 5:44). Loving our enemies is, in fact, one of the greatest weapons we can use against the real enemy. Recognizing our real enemy will help us to see the source of the conflict and to point our warfare accordingly. We are not fighting against people but against the forces of darkness. The apostle Paul described it like this:

> *For we do not wrestle against flesh and blood, but against principalities, against powers, against the rulers of the darkness of this age, against spiritual hosts of wickedness in the heavenly places.*
>
> —EPHESIANS 6:12 NKJV

Our spiritual enemy is real. Yet, God has promised that *"The God of peace will soon crush Satan under your feet"* (Rom. 16:20). The enemy's tactics against us will not prevail. Instead, God has commissioned us, by His power, to defeat the spiritual enemies in our lives. He has made us giant slayers, and under our feet the enemy will be crushed. He has given us the authority *"to overcome all the power of the enemy"* (Luke 10:19). In this way, God will actually turn all of the enemy's attempts against him, and what he thought would harm us will instead become a vehicle for our blessing and promotion. This is what the Bible means when it promises that *"in all things God works for the good of those who love him, who have been called according to his purpose"* (Rom. 8:28). God does not send giants to threaten us, but He uses every giant to bring us closer to our destiny.

Our enemies are yet another tool in the hand of God to enact His will in our lives. They are not meaningless obstacles or arbitrary challenges; they are opportunities to further the Kingdom and further ourselves in the Kingdom. Because of this, enemies are just as necessary and important to our lives as friends.

- Friends give us comfort, but enemies create change. The obstacles that enemies create force us to make decisions.

- Friends highlight our strengths, but enemies point to our weaknesses. They reveal the areas in which we need to grow.

- While friends support us, enemies reveal our limitations. By doing so, they actually motivate us to find the friends who will add true help and value to our lives. Thus, they keep us from isolation and bring us into greater unity with other believers. The presence of an enemy can also reveal who our true friends are.

- While friends believe in our destiny, enemies can move us from obscurity to prominence in a day. Life's rewards come from conquered enemies, and the size of our enemies determines the spoils of war. In a single day, Goliath turned David from a shepherd into a confidant of the king.

An enemy can give us in a day what a friend can give us in a lifetime. True challenge and experience are more valuable than gold—and these we gain from fighting our giants. For this reason, we should not despair when a giant shows up in our lives. It simply means the path to our promotion has just revealed itself. Every victory over a giant is followed by a reward.

ACCEPTING OUR REWARDS

After David killed Goliath, according to First Samuel 17:25, he received:

- Great riches

- Marriage to the king's daughter

- Exemption from taxes

- A place in the king's house

- Greater influence and responsibility

David received a reward. We often breeze past this portion of the story, but it is just as important as any other part. David's defeat of Goliath was met with tremendous reward, and David accepted it gladly. As giant slayers, we too must learn to receive the rewards that come with our victories. They are an important part of our destiny. Unfortunately, many Christians have a hard time receiving reward. Some think material blessing is evil. Others assume that reward will go to our heads and make us proud. These two lies have kept many believers from experiencing the rewards that God wants to give them.

The Lie of the Poverty Spirit

First, the lie of the poverty spirit has convinced many people that being poor is more spiritual and godly than being wealthy. In much of the Church, a stigma exists that says that those who have a lot of money must be sinful. The truth is, it is not what one has that makes one evil; it is what one loves that makes one evil. The Bible does not say that having money is evil, but that loving money leads to evil: *"For the love of money is a root of all kinds of evil"* (1 Tim. 6:10). This is a crucial distinction.

Much of the misunderstanding on this issue stems from the story of the rich young ruler in Mark 10. This man came to Jesus, telling him of all the things he had done to please God. He then asked, "What else should I do?" In response, Jesus told him to sell everything he had and give the money to the poor. After hearing this, the young man became sorrowful and realized that he loved money more than he loved God. The Bible says he walked away sad, leaving Jesus behind. Afterward, Jesus told His disciples that it is easier for a camel to go through the eye of a needle than for a rich person to enter the Kingdom of God. Jesus had identified the one thing in this young man's life that he loved more than God—money. Because money was an idol in this man's life, he needed to sell all in order to follow Jesus. But this is not true for all people everywhere.

Many Christians have misinterpreted Jesus' statement, thinking that it is impossible to be a Christian and be wealthy. Jesus did not say it was impossible for a rich person to be saved, only that it was more difficult. This is because when people have great riches and do not know Jesus, they have a tendency to become dependent on their financial standing and the lifestyle that their wealth provides. In order to accept Jesus, they have to make Him first in their lives.

However, if Jesus is first in our lives and we have cultivated generous hearts, God wants to make us conduits of His blessing in this world—not just spiritual blessing but also material blessing. He wants us to be rich so that we always have resources to be generous and, by doing so, to bring glory to God: *"You will be enriched in every way so that you can be generous on every occasion, and through us your generosity will result in thanksgiving to God"* (2 Cor. 9:11). God wants His Church to be the most generous people on the planet! He wants generosity to be a hallmark of His children. But, it is difficult to be generous when we are desperate and trying to just get by. This is one purpose of the rewards God loves to shower on us when we defeat the giants along our way.

The Lie of False Humility

The second lie, false humility, which masquerades as piety, tries to steal heavenly reward from God's servants by telling us it's wrong to be rewarded. In God's Kingdom, the opposite is true. We have a good Father who wants to reward us for serving Him and growing His Kingdom. It is actually a disservice to His love for us to deny the rewards He offers us—the rewards that are a natural result of our victories—in the name of protecting humility. Imagine if David had turned down the rewards King Saul offered him. If he had said, "Thanks, King Saul, but it would be wrong of me to receive these rewards. I'm just going to return to obscurity with my father's sheep," he would have insulted Saul. Further, he would have lost all the connections and influence that he had gained—the connections and influence that were crucial to his destiny. Thankfully, David knew it wasn't wrong to receive honor and reward. He recognized that the specific rewards connected to his victory over Goliath were positioning him for his future.

What we can learn from David is that humility is an inside job. David wasn't afraid of reward because his heart was pure. He knew, whether he had a lot or a little, whether he was famous or unknown, he would love and serve God with his whole heart. This is true humility. It is not defined by external actions but by our internal state. Anyone can appear to be humble, but true humility happens within. True humility will not be negatively affected by honor and reward. Instead, humility knows how to receive reward while remembering that the source of the strength to defeat the giant and the reward for doing so both come only from God. In His goodness, He rewards us for being faithful when we owe our ability to succeed completely to Him. True humility recognizes this and is able to freely enjoy the honor and rewards our Father gives as a demonstration of His love for and delight in us.

Just as God does not allow meaningless obstacles to come into our paths, He does not offer us meaningless rewards. Heavenly rewards are meant to motivate us to overcome our giants and to teach us about His Kingdom. We require great motivation to fight the battles ahead because as children of God we are called to fight and win against the impossible. The greater the impossibility and risk of our fight, the greater the reward He offers us.

RISK AND REWARD

On March 9, 2013, the world woke up to the report that a mob of radical Muslims had attacked the St. Joseph Colony, a community of Christians in Lahore, Pakistan. These Muslims had destroyed two hundred homes and eighty businesses—all belonging to Christians. Watching the reports of the devastation, I could feel the fear and anguish of that community, and I knew God was calling me to go. I realized I had to say *no* to everything else in order to say *yes* to this assignment. It was a big step of faith. Yes, it was a big risk financially, but even more so it was a risk of life. *Is this something I am willing to die for?* I asked myself.

Only a few weeks later, my team and I landed in Pakistan and were able to visit the St. Joseph Colony. We talked with people and walked through ruins. We were also able to meet with key Muslim and Christian leaders under the direction of Dr. Marqus Fida. We organized an opportunity for people to financially help those who had suffered from the attack. This led to us meeting at a hotel with four hundred religious and government leaders—all with the TV and newspaper reporters present. In unity, as Muslims and Christians, we came together to say *no* to such evil. Next, we organized a meeting at a stadium two hours away where we held a big healing festival. In the next three days, we saw thousands of healings, including many creative miracles. Most importantly, more than eighty-seven thousand people said *yes* to Jesus. What an incredible reward!

These eighty-seven thousand responses to the gospel were a significant milestone for me. On June 6, 1995, I received a prophetic word from Dr. Randy Clark that through my ministry I would see one million people saved. For almost twenty years, I had sacrificed and had focused on my assignment. I had poured out in pursuit of least, last, and the lost, and God had faithfully showed up in partnership with my obedience and willingness to be a giant slayer. In less than eighteen years, God had fulfilled that prophetic word with one million lives being transformed because I was willing to show up for battle.

Often since then, I have asked myself, *What if I was not willing to go? What if I had stayed at home from this battle? What if I had not shown up for any of these battles?* I had many other things I needed to do and deadlines to meet. Going to Pakistan in 2013, at that time, was not convenient or logical. It wasn't safe either. What if I was not willing to kiss my wife and kids goodbye and risk dying for what I believe? Or, what if I had not been willing to meet with those Muslim leaders? What would have happened to all those people? I am so thankful that God pushed me past the inconvenience and fear to see the potential for reward—in increased unity between Muslims and Christians, in souls saved, and in bodies healed. This potential drove me to take great risks in facing this giant. But the payoff was more than worth it. Often, the highest risks also have the highest rewards. Through my trip to Pakistan, the environment changed, and thousands of lives were impacted for the Kingdom. All that reward started when the environment in me started to change, and I decided to embrace the risk in pursuit of the reward. This event in Pakistan was one of biggest breakthroughs I have ever experienced, and it came as a result of taking a big risk.

We cannot deny the connection between reward and risk. To receive big rewards, we need to be willing to take big risks for God's Kingdom. David defeated Goliath because he wasn't afraid to attempt the impossible. If we want to be giant slayers like David, then we too have to become comfortable with attempting the impossible. All giants appear invincible until they are defeated. Risk and reward are inherently linked.

Every soldier in Saul's army was too afraid to fight Goliath, both in fear for their own lives and fear of the pain that would be brought on their comrades if they lost this key conflict. The rewards were apparent. Saul announced them to everyone, but no one was willing to take the risk needed to gain the rewards—until David arrived on the scene. David saw the need, heard about the reward, and embraced the risk as his pathway to victory.

We are called to do the same. Of course, it is not always easy to create the courage needed to take the risk. It wouldn't be risk if it felt easy. But, remembering the rewards God has placed on the other side of our victory will help. Doing so will help us position ourselves to take risk when the opportunity comes. And remembering that both the courage and the rewards come from God will help us to avoid seeking the victory only for the reward.

Positioned to Risk

One of the biggest keys to positioning ourselves for risk is refusing to take counsel from a pessimist. Faith is optimistic; it believes for the impossible because it believes that with God all things are possible (see Matt. 19:26). As mentioned in chapter 7, when we know we are called to fight a giant, the possibility of victory must be our focus, not the possibility of defeat. Saul and his soldiers were terrified of Goliath. All they saw was how difficult it would be to fight him. This made them bad counselors on how to defeat him. Thus, when David suggested that he could fight Goliath, Saul gave the classic pessimist answer: *"You are not able to go against this Philistine to fight with him; for you are but a youth while he has been a warrior from his youth"* (1 Sam. 17:33 NASB). Everyone told David, "Goliath's too big! We can't kill him." David said, "He's too big; I can't miss!"

When we decide to take a risk and try the impossible, people are guaranteed to tell us to give up. They will call us crazy for even thinking about trying, and they will point out all the reasons why we will fail. If we accept the pessimists' reasoning, believing the impossible is truly impossible, then we may as well give up from the start. This is why we must never receive counsel from pessimists. We can't let the opinions and failures of others determine our potential for success. Fear often tries to disguise itself as wisdom. This is more apparent in a pessimist than anywhere else. Though pessimists will surely come to us and speak their doom and gloom, we must choose, like David did, to ignore their fear and to embrace the risks of faith with a brave heart.

Winning for God

As we do this, it is important to also remember that when we fight giants, we always win for God and His Kingdom, not for our own glory or benefit. Some people love the thrill of risk-taking, and they may be driven to take risks and fight giants to build their own kingdoms. This is not a battle God will endorse. As we discussed in chapter 4, one of the keys to killing giants is aligning ourselves with God and His covenant. If we choose to step outside of His leading or to act for our own glory, we risk great defeat. After all, it is by His strength that we can gain the victory—not our own. David knew this well, and though he sought the reward of victory, he never lost sight of the fact that it was only by God's strength that he could win. Just before the conflict began, David said to Goliath:

> *You come against me with sword and spear and javelin, but I come against you in the name of the Lord Almighty, the God of the armies of Israel, whom you have defied. This day the Lord will deliver you into my hands, and I'll strike you down and cut off your head.*
>
> —1 SAMUEL 17:45-46

This is the sign of humility. David knew this conflict was not about him or his reward. Yes, he knew he would benefit greatly from following

God's call and taking the risk of faith, but ultimately this fight was about something much deeper. It was about defending God's honor among the nations, and it was about saving His people from an enemy. Because David recognized the true battle, he was able to humbly partner with God to bring God's victory to the situation. Though David was the one to take heart and courageously step on the field, he also recognized that God was fighting on his side. It was the Lord who would deliver Goliath into David's hands.

We cannot underestimate the importance of this confident humility. As we take great risks and win great battles, we must always remember these words from God—*"You will not succeed by your own strength or by your own power, but by my Spirit"* (Zech. 4:6 NCV). We were never meant to face our giants alone. We cannot overcome the impossible on our own. God's word encourages us to attempt great things and take great risks for Him—not in our own strength, but by the strength of God. David came against Goliath in the name of God—not in his own name. As a result, he won the victory, and he received a magnificent reward.

God is our ready partner in every battle. He calls us to the fight, He whispers His guidance in our ears, and He brings us peace with His presence. He is the one who shows us the path to victory. He is the one who takes our strength and adds His power. He is the one who set us up for victory from the start and then rewards us extravagantly when we win. Without God many things are impossible; with Him nothing is impossible. With this in view, we must ask ourselves, *Why wouldn't I take great faith risks in obedience to God's call?* When we are tempted to shy away from the battle, we must remember the rewards that wait for us on the other side of victory—the lives changed, the atmospheres shifted, the provision accessed, the prayers answered, the destiny fulfilled.

QUESTIONS TO PONDER

1. As we move toward our assignment, giants will block the road ahead. Think about the giants that lie between you and your destiny. Now ask yourself, *Could this be the very thing God will use to promote me?* Name the giants that are standing in your way, and ask the Holy Spirit to show you how He will use their defeat to promote you. Write down what you hear.

    _____

    _____

    _____

    _____

    _____

    _____

    _____

    _____

    _____

2. Have you ever refused to accept reward? What caused you to do this? What needs to shift in your heart and mind so that you can freely accept the rewards He wants to give you?

    _____

    _____

    _____

    _____

    _____

    _____

    _____

3. Are there people in your life who are opposing you and your destiny? If so, how can you respond to the person in love while battling the spiritual forces that are opposing you?

_____

_____

_____

_____

_____

_____

_____

_____

DECLARATION

Today I declare that I will embrace risk in faith, and I will seek God's rewards for victory. These rewards are not evil, and they will not cause me to stumble or become proud. Instead, they will position me for promotion into my destiny and provide the resources I need to build God's Kingdom. I declare that my life will be characterized by great risk, great victory, and great reward—all for God's glory!

PART 3

TAKING THE VICTORY

RULE 9

BE YOURSELF

Then Saul dressed David in his own tunic. He put a coat of armor on him and a bronze helmet on his head. David fastened on his sword over the tunic and tried walking around, because he was not used to them. "I cannot go in these," he said to Saul, "because I am not used to them." So he took them off. Then he took his staff in his hand, chose five smooth stones from the stream, put them in the pouch of his shepherd's bag and, with his sling in his hand, approached the Philistine.

—1 SAMUEL 17:38–40

King Saul, after listening to David's stories of his previous victories over the lion and the bear, agreed to allow David to fight Goliath. We don't know for sure whether he was fully convinced that David was the man for the job or whether he agreed simply because David was his only volunteer. Regardless, we know Saul believed David—the shepherd boy dressed in a simple tunic and armed with only a sling—needed some help. He was not outfitted like a true warrior. According to earthly wisdom, someone who was going to face a warrior as fearsome and skilled as Goliath should be equipped with the best weapons and armor available. Saul was an experienced warrior, and he was applying that experience to the current situation. He knew David needed better armor and weapons, so he dressed him in his.

However, when David tried on the armor, he found that it didn't fit. Saul was a grown man and David was just a boy. Further, David was a shepherd, not a soldier. He was not accustomed to the weight and limited movement that accompanied armor. Wearing armor would have made him safer in some ways, but it also would have limited his ability to move quickly, which was his greatest strength. In the end, David realized that the protection offered by the armor was greatly outweighed by the protection that came from operating in his own anointing. David rejected the armor and chose, instead, to focus on playing to his strengths and anointing. The lesson here may seem obvious, but it is nonetheless essential. We cannot walk in someone else's anointing.

When the prophet Samuel had anointed David as the future king, it was not just a symbolic act. It was a spiritual impartation, *"and the Spirit of the Lord came upon David from that day forward"* (1 Sam. 16:13 NKJV). This was key to David's success. He had a unique kingly anointing from God, and he needed to walk in it. The last thing God wanted David to do was walk in the anointing of Saul—the king God had rejected. No, David needed to be himself, and by doing so he would tap into the power of God.

Not only was wearing Saul's armor outside David's sweet spot, but it also was outside God's plan for the fight. Saul had David's best interest in mind, but he was acting with the wisdom of people and not the wisdom of God. By doing so, he would have turned God's supernatural solution into a natural one. If David had gone on the battlefield in Saul's armor, it would have sabotaged what God was trying to do. David was not appointed by God to defeat Goliath because he was a great warrior; he was appointed because he was a shepherd. The giant was well known for defeating warriors. A warrior was not what was needed.

It took wisdom and confidence for David to recognize that being himself and using his unique gifts and experience would be more effective than trying to fit into the mold that seemed more appropriate for the fight. David did not fit the mold, and as it turns out, that is exactly what enabled him to succeed. I am convinced that if David had gone out on that battlefield wearing Saul's armor he would not have returned alive. Thankfully, David recognized Saul's mistake and chose to approach the problem the way God had taught him while he was a shepherd.

MADE TO SUCCEED

Like David, each one of us is uniquely made to succeed in the battles we are assigned to fight. We must learn to believe this. God made us to succeed. We have what it takes, because of His Spirit within us and because of the gifts and abilities He created us with. This is the two-fold empowerment that every giant slayer has.

First, we must understand that, as children of God, we are just as equipped to succeed as any other believer. We cannot look at other Christians and think, *If I was more gifted like him or had her experiences, then I could face this giant.* The truth is, it is the Spirit who enables and prepares us, and He lives in our hearts. By His Spirit, God has given each one of us His specialized armor. None of us are without it. Unlike Saul's armor, this spiritual armor is a perfect fit and weight, and when we wear it, it enables us to *"stand against the devil's schemes"* (Eph. 6:11). Paul describes God's armor in Ephesians 6:

> *Stand firm then, with the belt of truth buckled around your waist, with the breastplate of righteousness in place, and with*

> *your feet fitted with the readiness that comes from the gospel of*
> *peace. In addition to all this, take up the shield of faith, with*
> *which you can extinguish all the flaming arrows of the evil*
> *one. Take the helmet of salvation and the sword of the Spirit,*
> *which is the word of God.*
>
> —EPHESIANS 6:14-17

This armor of the Spirit gives us the advantage we need to win against the giants of our lives. Without God's Spirit, we are helpless. Thankfully, we have each been given the Holy Spirit to teach and guide us. We have been adopted into the Kingdom of God through the blood of Jesus. We have been given an identity that means something in Heaven and in hell. When we feel unequal to the task ahead of us, we do not need to worry; the presence of the Holy Spirit will fill in the gaps until we are more than enough to conquer any challenge.

Second, we must understand that God has used our circumstances, personalities, gifts, and anointing to uniquely prepare us to defeat the giants we face. Because of this, we are actually the most qualified people to fight these giants. It can be easy to look at the circumstances of our lives and feel that it is impossible for us to overcome them. We may feel that a better or stronger person would be able to deal with our giants— maybe someone who looks a certain way or has particular skills. But this is not the way God works. God has uniquely crafted each one of us to defeat every giant that comes along our paths.

If we feel like success is unlikely, we must remember that God loves to use unlikely heroes. He loves to take the foolish and weak things of this world and use them in a way that confounds the wise (see 1 Cor. 1:27). Though we may not look the part, we can trust that, as He did with David, God has prepared and equipped us perfectly for our battles. We are uniquely prepared us to be victorious as giant slayers. Our identity is linked to our victory. When we embrace who we are and who God made us to be, we unlock our destiny. When we, like David, become comfortable with being ourselves, we are most ready to defeat the giants in our own way.

Then, no matter what giants stand in the way of our destiny, we can confidently approach them as ourselves. We will not feel the pressure to be like someone else because we will understand that we are God's special weapon in this particular fight. This giant would not be in our path if we were not meant to overcome it. When giants show up in our lives, it is because we are the ones appointed to overcome them. It is our own unique anointing that has qualified us to do so. No matter the situation, who we are is the most powerful person we can be.

WALTZING IN OUR OWN ANOINTING

A few years ago, I was invited to speak at a relatively large church in Ohio. I had been teaching at a conference the previous two days, and it had gone well. People received the words the Holy Spirit had given me, and many were set free and healed. I expected this church service to be no different. What I didn't know was that God had something special up His sleeve—and He wanted to use my unique anointing and personality to bring an unexpected breakthrough.

When we arrived, I noticed that the atmosphere in the sanctuary felt a little reserved. The finely dressed members of the congregation entered the room with solemn expressions on their faces. All the leaders addressed each other by their formal titles, and the service proceeded precisely on schedule. I have no problem with formality in the church. It can hold a kind of reverence that other sorts of churches sometimes lose in the pursuit of freedom. To disregard either side is to deny what I believe to be legitimate and essential aspects of God's personality. Instead, it is our responsibility to recognize what the Holy Spirit is emphasizing—whether the quiet reverence that comes from formality or the release of freedom that comes from less traditional forms of worship.

After the worship, the head pastor approached the pulpit to introduce me. As he did, I felt the Holy Spirit whisper in my ear, "I want you to lay down." I was apprehensive at first. This was clearly not appropriate for the setting. I was supposed to be speaking in about fifteen seconds. But I know my Father's voice and have learned to obey it without question. So I laid down on the stage. The pastor finished his introduction and stepped away from the pulpit, expecting me to stand up.

Expectation can be tricky when it comes to ministry. On one hand, it is important to meet people where they are. Jesus used simple stories and illustrations to share the gospel with the people who followed Him. On the other hand, it is important to avoid lowering the standard of God's Kingdom to meet people's expectations. Jesus also occasionally shared revelations and teachings that caused everyone listening to disperse and His disciples to question Him. Pastors will sometimes tell me what they expect me to share before I speak at a church. It is, of course, my desire to honor them, but sometimes to do so would violate my relationship with the Spirit. I have, in the past, stifled the message the Lord gave me to accommodate the wishes of leaders. It never once paved the way for great breakthrough, and I repented to the Holy Spirit every time. It was those experiences that made me stay down with my face on the floor.

I could feel the awkwardness growing around me as the dead silence wore on. This was not a normal occurrence at this church. In fact, based on the way the anxiety was growing in the room, I guessed these people may have never seen someone laid out under the power of the anointing. But I did not feel the release from the Spirit, so I did not stand. As the unease reached its peak, the pastor took the pulpit again, suggesting that my assistant come up and speak for a moment. She stood, sharing about some of the fruit that we'd seen in recent years, as well as a few of her own personal testimonies. She returned to her seat after she had said all that she could think to say, and still I remained laid out on the stage, unmoving.

Now the tension in the room reached a new height. I could feel it prickling on my back and neck like electricity. Though a part of me felt guilty for not meeting everyone's expectations, the warmth of the Holy Spirit was filling me so fully that I didn't care. Finally, the pastor returned to the pulpit to close the service. I remember looking at his brown shoes as he stood next to me, the odd angle giving me a uniquely clear view of them. I heard the Holy Spirit again as I looked, "Touch his shoes." So I did. The moment my fingers brushed the top of the brown leather the pastor fell flat on his back, knocked over by the power of the Spirit.

The entire congregation gasped, and one woman let out a little scream. After it became clear that the pastor was not going to immediately return to his feet, one of the other leaders climbed up the stage to help and then promptly fell down next to the pastor. Another person came to help, and another. Soon there were nearly a dozen people laid out across the stage in various positions. Then I felt the Holy Spirit release me to stand.

The attitude of the crowd was mixed. One third were rushing to the front of the room to receive what the Spirit was releasing, another third were sitting in their chairs with crossed arms and scowls on their faces, and the rest seemed like they couldn't decide between excitement and concern. Feeling the intoxicating warmth of the presence of God flowing through my chest, I grabbed the microphone and shared the words that the Holy Spirit had placed on my heart. I said, "The rhythm of heaven is in the waltz."

Everyone—angry, happy, or otherwise—turned and looked at one another. Each expression said the same thing, "What does that have to do with anything?"

Then, compelled by God's presence, I began to dance the waltz, humming as I did. I went through my little tune three times, careful not to step on any of the fallen church leaders as I danced. Looks of confusion and frustration were written on most of the faces that watched me as I danced. Then the presence of God fell on the whole room, a tangible and warm sensation of peace and joy. Some danced, some fell under the power, and some simply stood in awe of the goodness they felt.

I danced off the stage and into the aisle, touching people as I felt the Spirit compel me. One man, still with an angry look on his face, stood as I approached. He cocked back a clenched fist and moved in close to take a swing at me. But he dropped to the floor once he got within a few feet, overwhelmed by the sense of love and joy that was flooding the room. The meeting went on like that for a long time, a palpable sense of love flooding every corner of the room. Many were touched and many were healed of sickness and pain, not because anyone prayed for them, but just because the love of God had come to visit with us.

It all began with my willingness to be myself and to not fit the mold when God was doing something different. Learning to be ourselves can be intimidating. There may be times when we have to do things differently than what is considered normal. David was denying traditional wisdom by going to fight a battle-hardened soldier in a simple tunic. I was denying traditional wisdom by spending the first half of my sermon lying down on the floor and the second half doing the waltz. God likes to work with the original and the unconventional because He is original and unconventional.

People may try to put us in a box with their expectations. This usually is not because of any ill intent, but because they want what they are accustomed to. They want normal. God, however, has called us to be more than normal. To reach the heights of victory that God has planned for us, we must be willing to go outside the comfort of normalcy. One of the biggest problems with normalcy is that it discounts the unique anointing that God has placed on each of our lives. It tries to fit us in a mold when God didn't use a mold to make us. When we try to fit a mold instead of listening to God's voice and walking in our unique anointing, we are in danger of trying to fight our battles apart from the anointing. This is a mistake we do not want to make. Instead, we must be willing to fully embrace who He has made us to be, uniquely, and play to the strengths of our gifts and anointing.

FINDING FRESH OIL

This is possible, of course, only when we are filled with the presence of God. Who we are is inseparably connected to who He is and what He has done in us. Because of this, as giant slayers we must be careful to never lose our value for the presence of God. We must never become so confident in our anointing and the battles we've already won that we stop spending time in God's presence. His presence is everything. Jesus came and died so that we could be in the presence of our Father, God. It is in this place of knowing and being known by God that we receive our anointing and the wisdom we need for every battle. This is why David was able to defeat Goliath. He had spent years in God's presence, worshiping with his harp as he tended the sheep. As a result, he knew his unique anointing, and he arrived at the battle full of God's presence. This made him confident when he accepted Goliath's challenge and confident that he did not need someone else's armor to do it.

David knew who he was and what he was capable of because he was filled with God's presence. He also knew that one moment of anointing in the presence of God is not enough. It would not work for him to enter his first battle in the anointing and then think he could manage the rest on his own. Instead, David made spending time in God's presence his greatest pursuit. Whether he was in the fields with the sheep, hiding out in caves, or ruling from the palace, his first priority was knowing God. The same must be true for us. Encounters with God must become a part of our lifestyle. We need to be filled and anointed again and again so that we are reminded of who we are in Him and what He has called us to do. We need to have fresh oil.

After years of seeing the faithfulness of God, David continued to voice his need for fresh oil so that he could be fully himself and bear fruit in his old age:

> *You have exalted my horn like that of a wild ox; fine oils have been poured on me. My eyes have seen the defeat of my adversaries; my ears have heard the rout of my wicked foes. The righteous will flourish like a palm tree, they will grow like a cedar of Lebanon; planted in the house of the Lord, they will flourish in the courts of our God. They will still bear fruit in old age, they will stay fresh and green, proclaiming, "The Lord is upright; he is my Rock, and there is no wickedness in him."*
>
> —Psalm 92:10-15

Like David, we need a daily outpouring of God's presence in our hearts; we need to be anointed with the fine oils of Heaven. While spending time in God's presence is important simply for our relationship with Him, when it comes to fighting our giants this fresh oil has two primary benefits. First, every day holds new challenges, and we need a fresh encounter to prepare us for these new challenges. Yesterday's anointing was the anointing for yesterday. It is not sufficient for today. If we rely on yesterday's encounters for today's battles, we will soon become weary. We do not have what we need to fight on our own. Only by His presence and His anointing are we able to live as the giant slayers He has made us to be.

Second, we need fresh encounters in the presence of God because they heighten our spiritual sensitivity. We see this in David's statement—*"My eyes have seen the defeat of my adversaries; my ears have heard the rout of my wicked foes."* Through spending time with God, David was able to discern God's plans for victory, and his faith was stirred to believe that his enemies would be defeated. Like David, when we are filled daily with God's presence and anointing, our spiritual eyes and ears will be open, and we will live with greater spiritual awareness and sensitivity. Fresh oil illuminates God's strategies and enables us to have victory over our enemies.

If we want to succeed in fighting our giants, we must remember the power of being ourselves and embracing who God has made us to be. Recognizing the unique call and anointing on our lives brings us the spiritual knowledge, endurance, and strength we need to complete the tasks before us. To do this, we must daily enter God's presence and invite the daily anointing of His fresh oil. There is no other way to be fully ourselves. There is no other way to be fully prepared. We see this in Psalm 23, where David speaks of his quiet and refreshing times in God's presence—*"He makes me lie down in green pastures, he leads me beside quiet waters"* (Ps. 23:2). Because he had cultivated a lifestyle of encounter, David also knew how to fellowship with God even in the darkest valley and in the presence of his enemies (see Ps. 23:4). Even in those places, David could say, *"You anoint my head with oil; my cup overflows"* (Ps. 23:5).

This is the key to walking in our own anointing and being victorious in all situations. We must learn to live a lifestyle of encountering God and walking in our anointing *before* we are faced with a giant. It is one thing to shout out a panicked prayer when a crisis arrives. It is quite another to enter a crisis full of the confidence and clarity that comes from time spent in God's presence. When he stepped on the battlefield to face Goliath, David knew exactly who he was and what he carried. He had become familiar with the presence of God in the field with the sheep. He became familiar with the sling as well. Because he knew who he was, it was easy for him to see that Saul's armor was not a good fit. He was not a trained warrior; he was an experienced shepherd. A trained warrior probably would have lost the battle with Goliath. Goliath knew how to fight warriors; he had probably never fought a shepherd before. Being himself was crucial to David's success.

The same is true for us. To win against our giants, we must be comfortable walking in our own unique anointing. To do that, we must spend time daily in God's presence, where we are reminded of who we are and what we carry. As we regularly connect with Him, we will become familiar with the unique tools He has given us. Then, when our battles come, we will be ready to fight as ourselves. God knows who we are and what we can do, and He has prepared us to defeat the giants we face—not masquerading as anyone else but confidently walking as ourselves.

QUESTIONS TO PONDER

1. David was just a youth and the least of his brothers. This could have easily made him feel disqualified when he faced the giant Goliath. What areas of your life make you feel unqualified? Are these just the result of cultural norms or something else?

_____

_____

_____

_____

_____

_____

2. Why did Saul try to fit his armor on David? What do you think his motives were?

_____

_____

_____

_____

_____

_____

3. How has God uniquely gifted and prepared you to fight certain giants? What steps can you take to be more truly yourself and to walk in your own anointing?

_____

_____

_____

_____

_____

_____

4. Is entering God's presence easy for you? Take five minutes and sit quietly, focusing on God's presence. What did He tell you? What did you feel?

_____

_____

_____

_____

_____

5. Identify time each day this week when you can prioritize spending time with God. Write down one question to ask God about your anointing each day.

_____

_____

_____

_____

_____

DECLARATION

God has uniquely and specially created me as a giant slayer. He has given me His Spirit and His supernatural armor, and He has also given me unique gifts and anointing. I do not need to be like anyone else to succeed. Instead, I need to be who God created me to be, even if that looks different from the norm. As I daily spend time with God, He will teach me about who I am and what I am equipped to do. He has made me capable for every assignment in my life.

RULE 10

BRING THE RIGHT WEAPONS

Then he took his staff in his hand, chose five smooth stones from
the stream, put them in the pouch of his shepherd's bag and, with
his sling in his hand, approached the Philistine.

—1 SAMUEL 17:40

Every battle requires a weapon. Not all weapons are created equal, however. The giant Goliath had the typical weapons of a warrior—a bronze javelin, a spear, and a sword, as well as a massive shield and body armor. But because of his tremendous size, his weapons were super-sized. Just the tip of his spear weighed fifteen pounds. This made fighting him even more challenging. By comparison, David's weapons—a staff, a sling, and a handful of stones—probably seemed ridiculous. Most would not have seen this as a wise way to attack an experienced and heavily armed soldier. Even Saul felt it necessary to equip the young shepherd boy with heavy armor and weapons. Yet, as we discussed in the last chapter, David rejected Saul's armor and chose to approach the battle using his own unique gifts—the slinging skills of a shepherd.

When Goliath saw a youth answering his challenge with no armor and a poor excuse for weapons, he was outraged. The Israelites had not sent out their best warrior, but only an impudent youth without a proper weapon. In Goliath's eyes, it was both a joke and an insult:

> Meanwhile, the Philistine, with his shield bearer in front of him, kept coming closer to David. He looked David over and saw that he was little more than a boy, glowing with health and handsome, and he despised him. He said to David, "Am I a dog, that you come at me with sticks?" And the Philistine cursed David by his gods.
>
> —I SAMUEL 17:41-43

To Goliath, it seemed as though David was coming out to fight him with a stick. It's not clear whether Goliath saw the sling and pouch of stones David also carried. It's reasonable to think he may have missed them, considering the smallness of these weapons and the distance between the warriors. What Goliath most likely overlooked was, in fact, the surprise weapon that enabled David to win.

A SURPRISE STRATEGY

Many people do not realize that the sling was actually a common weapon, similar to the bow and arrow, in ancient warfare. Because of this, we have viewed David's weapons as a disadvantage when, in fact, they were exactly what he needed for a surprise attack. The long-range sling was the only weapon that could actually win against Goliath. David (and everyone else) knew that engaging Goliath in hand-to-hand combat was a recipe for death. But only David had the skills needed to take Goliath down before Goliath was close enough to use his weapons.

Sling stones could be hurled over 1,500 feet at speeds as fast as 250 miles per hour, depending on the skill of the slinger. Imagine the impact of an egg-sized stone flung at that speed with great precision. In many ways, it was the ancient equivalent of a bullet. Often, slingers were used to send large volleys of stones upon the enemy from a distance. However, skilled slingers were also known for incredible accuracy in hitting a target head-on (like David did). In fact, prior to David's day, the tribe of Benjamin was known for having an elite corps of slingers, *"each of whom could sling a stone at a hair and not miss"* (Judg. 20:16).

Slingers had several advantages over archers. They could fire and reload more quickly, and they could hit targets at greater distances. Also, a sling and stones are much easier to make and maintain, are less cumbersome in battle, and are easier to hide than a bow and arrows. Slingers are also more able to fire while on the move, as David did. A sling in the hands of a skilled slinger like David was the best personal long-range weapon in the ancient world. It is not surprising, then, that archeologists have found large numbers of sling stones in excavation sites in Israel and other parts of the ancient world.[1]

It seems likely that slinging played a significant role in the warfare of ancient Israel (see 2 Kings 3:25), but we don't know much about the advent of slinging in Israel or whether Saul had made use of slingers in his army. We do know that many of the men who followed and fought for David in later years, while he fled from Saul, were expert slingers: *"They were armed with bows and were able to shoot arrows or to sling stones right-handed or left-handed"* (1 Chron. 12:2). Perhaps David's victory over Goliath brought the sling to prominence as a weapon. Regardless, it seems clear that in the face-off with Goliath, David was the only one who considered the strategic impact of the sling.

David had, after all, spent years defending his father's sheep with a sling, and through daily practice he had become very skilled at it. Training and preparation are required each time God moves us forward in our destiny. For David, his training and diligence with a shepherd's sling was crucial to his victory on the battlefield. When the battle came, David did not choose a sling and a stone at random. He chose those weapons because they were the weapons he had trained with. They were his sweet spot, and he was about to show the world how good he had become.

David knew how to load and sling the stone while running forward. This gave him the ultimate chance at a surprise attack. Before Goliath knew what was coming, he had been hit. Further, David was experienced enough to accurately aim for the only part of Goliath's body that was not covered with armor and to gauge the exact timing and distance needed to take down the giant before he was in range of his spear. Timing was everything. Once Goliath was close enough to use his spear, David's chances of success dwindled. David took five stones with him, knowing he might need more than one shot, but the first shot mattered most. With God's help, David used his skills and experience as a slinger to hit Goliath hard enough with the first shot. Goliath fell face forward, and David then used Goliath's sword to kill him. On the day he battled Goliath, David's skill was married with God's anointing, and the giant was defeated.

David's success here shows us the vital importance of bringing the right weapon to the battle. David knew his anointing and his ability. He rejected Saul's weapons and chose the weapon he was skilled in using, recognizing the unique advantages—surprise and long-range accuracy—this weapon presented in this battle against the "unbeatable giant." Because of this, David was able to succeed where everyone else would have failed. He was uniquely gifted to defeat his giant, and so are we. To utilize our unique advantage like David did, we need to make sure we are using the right weapon for the battle. The way we choose to engage our giants is just as important as whether or not we choose to engage our giants. The wrong weapon may bring harm to us or those around us. It may be a hindrance when it is meant to be a help.

CHOOSING THE RIGHT WEAPON

David won a physical battle using a surprising weapon that was uniquely suited to defeat the giant he faced. As we fight spiritual battles, the secret to our success is often found in using an unexpected or seemingly illogical weapon. Though it doesn't make sense to human reasoning, it is in fact God's strategy for victory. I discovered the truth of this in a powerful way during a ministry trip in Pakistan. In the Spirit, I was up against a towering giant, and it looked like it was impossible to succeed. Yet, God gave me a surprise strategy that defied conventional wisdom and involved a good bit of risk. But as He did with David, He stood by my side and enabled my surprise weapon to win a tremendous victory.

It happened several years ago. I was lying in the back of a car in Pakistan, trying not to throw up. My body was covered in hives, I felt nauseated, and I had a splitting headache. I had just finished a phone call with one of my assistants, trying to sort out an issue with our computer systems back home that was causing massive financial problems. Several of our team members had also gotten sick, and we had received more threats of violence on this trip than any other I had ever been on. Despite all this, I was supposed to go on stage in fifteen minutes to preach the gospel to several thousand Muslims. We had built the stage especially for this occasion. This one meeting represented the culmination of months of work and numerous trials.

As I lay there, trying to remain composed, I knew I was not going to let the enemy get the victory. Despite my discomfort and all the oppression, I knew God had us there for a reason, and I was not willing to let anything undo that purpose. With help from one of the team members, I climbed out of the car and walked up the stairs to the stage. The crowd stretched out as far as I could see. Immediately, I could feel the tension in the sea of people that stood before me. It felt like a pot of water threatening to boil over.

I had done meetings in the Muslim world before. I was no stranger to this atmosphere, and we were prepared. Over one hundred and fifty guards were present to ensure the safety of my team and all others present. We had set up a rope barrier fifty feet in front of the stage, with guards maintaining the line to prevent any aggressors from rushing the stage. I had seen these kinds of meetings go badly in the past. Some Muslims are raised to hate and fear westerners, especially Christians. On more than one occasion, I had needed to be rushed from the stage and into a getaway car, and I worried this night might end in the same way.

I did not need to wait long to find out. My head still pounding, I watched as a sudden swell of people from the middle of the crowd surged forward, pushing through and knocking down the rope barrier. Their faces were twisted with looks of hate and disgust. The security guards did their best to stop the sudden flow of people, but the flood had come too quickly. I had thirty seconds to make a decision. To be honest, I didn't even really have time to think. I turned and looked at my event coordinator, who was looking for me to give the signal to pull us out and get us to safety. Feeling the tug of the Spirit on my heart, I looked at her and shook my head *no*. The second I did this, a presence descended upon the crowd like I had never before experienced. It was as if love Himself had come down and began radiating through all of us.

Love was God's surprise weapon that day. When I listened to His nudging and chose to stay, I brought the weapon of God's love to the battle, and hatred was no match for it. The aggressors stopped dead in their tracks, their expressions changing instantly before my eyes from looks of anger and disdain to joy and peace. Immediately everyone started dancing. They waved their arms back and forth, jumping and spinning around. I had never seen such jubilant worship anywhere in the Muslim world. As this happened, in an instant the headache, hives, and nausea left my body.

Over twenty-two thousand Muslims experienced the love of Jesus that night, and I saw some of the most profound creative miracles of my life.

Blind men and women had their sight restored. Children who had been paralyzed since birth began to walk. Deaf ears were opened. Tumors disintegrated. It was glorious. I had always known that the love of God was powerful, but that was the first time I had seen it stop a wave of hate in its tracks.

On the drive back after the meeting, I began to reflect on all the different ways the meeting could have gone. I could have cancelled or postponed because of my illness and the trouble back home. Or, we could have been escorted to safety as soon as the crowd turned aggressive. Instead, we listened to God's divine strategy and engaged His weapon of choice. We brought the right weapon to that particular battle, and as a result we experienced a significant victory.

When facing the giants of life, it is essential that we let the Spirit guide us in choosing the appropriate weapon for each battle. Sometimes we must engage in warfare, and sometimes we must fight with peace. Sometimes we must fight with confrontation, and sometimes we must fight with humor. Sometimes we fight with strategy, and sometimes we fight with artistic creativity. David chose to fight his battle against Goliath with stones instead of a sword. But in other battles, later in his life, he did use a sword. God gave Moses a staff so he could fight pharaoh's oppression with miracles. Solomon used the wealth and wisdom he had received from God to fight his battles. Jesus fought most of His battles with words.

We are all called to overcome different kinds of giants, and that means we all need different types of weapons. The key to victory is recognizing the Spirit's strategic weapon for each battle. He knows what will be most effective, even if it seems like the wrong approach to us. We must trust Him to reveal the weapons we need to overcome the giants we face.

Our Spiritual Arsenal

We also need to be familiar with the various weapons in our arsenal. David chose five stones and a sling as his weapons in the fight against Goliath, and he used these weapons expertly. However, he also recognized that the battle was a spiritual battle with spiritual weapons, and he owed his victory to God. David knew his success was ultimately linked to spiritual realities. This is why he so confidently told Goliath:

> *This day the Lord will deliver you into my hands.... All those gathered here will know that it is not by sword or spear that the Lord saves; for the battle is the Lord's, and he will give all of you into our hands.*
>
> —1 SAMUEL 17:46-47

It is not by sword or spear that God saves, but through His spiritual power. David's true weapons were not physical but spiritual. David carried something that made him run to the battle with the giant, not away from it. He had the courage to make his case to a king and the valor to convince him. David had everything he needed to defeat Goliath the moment he arrived at the battleground.

In this book, we've looked closely at David's character and choices, the quality of His connection to God, and his heart of courage. All of the ground rules in this book are spiritual weapons when placed in submission to God's leading. Without restating what we've already covered, I want to examine three key types of spiritual weapons that God has given us.

1. The Sword of the Spirit

The first type of spiritual weapon we have is the weapon of the word. The armor of God listed in Ephesians 6, which we looked at in the last chapter, contains only one weapon—the sword of the Spirit, *"which is the word of God"* (Eph. 6:17). The word of God, both the Scripture and the words we receive personally from the Spirit, is a key weapon in every fight.

A large part of why David had the confidence to face Goliath when everyone else was terrified was his knowledge of God's word. David knew the Scripture of his day, which contained the covenant God had with Israel. He knew the promises God had made to Israel regarding victory over their enemies, and this gave him confidence in facing Goliath, who was openly mocking God and His people. In David we see that being familiar with God's history with humanity creates a readiness and willingness to be a part of what God is doing now. It brings balance and solidity to every thought, as well as confidence to every action.

From David's psalms, we know David held the word of God in very high regard. About it, David said, *"How can a young person stay on the path of purity? By living according to your word,"* and, *"Oh, how I love your law! I meditate on it all day long. Your commands are always with me and make me wiser than my enemies"* (Ps. 119:9, 97-98). Looking back on the many battles of his life, David recognized that the word of God played a key role in making him wiser than his enemies. The writer of Hebrews also refers to the word of God as a sword that cuts through to the truth and brings understanding:

> *For the word of God is alive and active. Sharper than any double-edged sword, it penetrates even to dividing soul and spirit, joints and marrow; it judges the thoughts and attitudes of the heart.*
>
> —HEBREWS 4:12

David believed that living according to God's word was a powerful spiritual weapon that would give him the wisdom and strategy he needed to be victorious.

Of course, David not only knew the Scripture, but he also knew the personal prophetic word God had spoken to him through Samuel. Because of the prophecies over his own life, he was confident that God would give him success. When we, like David, immerse ourselves in God's word, we will be better equipped for battle. The truths of the Bible and God's prophecies over our lives are powerful spiritual weapons that will help us overcome the giants we face.

2. *The Fruit of the Spirit*

Our second type of spiritual weapon is the type I used on my trip to Pakistan—the weapon of the fruit of God's Spirit. In Galatians 5:22-23 we find a list of the powerful fruit that the Spirit bears in our lives: love, joy, peace, patience, kindness, goodness, faithfulness, gentleness, and self-control. As we are filled with the Spirit of God and begin to walk in our new creation identity, we begin to act more and more like our Father. We begin to demonstrate His character, which is a powerful contrast to the forces of evil in this world. Where the enemy brings fear, hatred, despair, impatience, cruelty, betrayal, greed, pride, and so forth, God offers the opposite. He offers love, joy, peace, and all the others. And God's nature always triumphs. His love is stronger.

This is the warfare strategy the apostle Paul highlights in Romans 12 when he says:

> *Do not take revenge, my dear friends, but leave room for God's wrath, for it is written: "It is mine to avenge; I will repay," says the Lord. On the contrary: "If your enemy is hungry, feed him; if he is thirsty, give him something to drink. In doing this, you will heap burning coals on his head." Do not be overcome by evil, but overcome evil with good.*
>
> —ROMANS 12:19-21

We, as God's image-bearers, get to step in and display the nature of God in hopeless situations. We get to overcome evil with good. This is a major part of how we fight the giants of this world. Where we see anger, we step in with forgiveness and love. Where we see greed, we step in with self-control and generosity. When we see evil, we step in with goodness and truth. As we become more and more like our Father, we ourselves become a weapon against the negative fruit of the enemy's kingdom. And through us, love gains the victory.

3. The Vision of the Spirit

The third type of spiritual weapon is vision. How we look at a giant determines what we see, and what we see determines our response. When David looked at Goliath, he did not see an impossible giant because he saw that God was bigger than the giant. He saw Goliath with God's vision, and as a result he knew Goliath could be overcome. Because he was full of the spirit, David was able to see past the external appearance of Goliath and see the will of God. Spiritual vision, simple as it may be, is a powerful weapon. Many giants have remained standing for generations simply because no one has been able to envision a world without them. Many of the Israelites died in the desert after leaving slavery in Egypt because they could not imagine the destiny that was ahead of them. It is as the proverb says: *"Where there is no vision, the people perish"* (Prov. 29:18 KJV). But when we see with God's eyes, we have the wisdom and understanding needed to discern God's strategy and defeat our giants.

THE POWER OF GOD'S WEAPONS

Lastly, in order to choose the right weapon for our battles, we need to believe that God's weapons are the most powerful choice. If we do not really believe this, we will be tempted to try to figure it out on our own. We'll resort to human measures, when only the measures of the Kingdom will work. God's weapons are very different from the weapons of this world. Paul makes this clear in his discussion of the Christian's warfare:

> *For though we live in the world, we do not wage war as the world does. The weapons we fight with are not the weapons of the world. On the contrary, they have divine power to demolish strongholds. We demolish arguments and every pretension that sets itself up against the knowledge of God, and we take captive every thought to make it obedient to Christ.*
>
> —2 CORINTHIANS 10:3-5

Instead of the world's natural weapons, we use spiritual weapons that are sourced in another realm. Both spiritual and supernatural, these weapons are more powerful than anything in this world or any force of evil. They are able to overthrow spiritual strongholds—both within the minds of people and over circumstances and regions. They can destroy thoughts and arguments against the existence and knowledge of God. In other words, they are powerful enough to bring people into encounters with God and overcome the lies that have kept them from receiving salvation. This is true spiritual power, and no weapon of the enemy can stand against us when we wield God's weapons and follow His battle strategy.

The enemy tries to tempt us into fighting with the wrong weapon. He tries to trick us into thinking that love is weak and peace is easily trampled on. He has to do this because the weapons that God gives us are so much more powerful than his. God's weapons are not meant to go toe to toe with the weapons of the enemy; they are designed to trump them. Goliath was no match for the expert shepherd slinger, and the forces of darkness are no match for the sons and daughters of God. Peace, love, courage, and kindness completely overcome the worst the enemy has to offer. All we need to do to avoid being tricked into using the weapons of this world is to remember that God's weapons are much stronger. With God's weapons, we can win every battle without a drop of blood being spilled.

NOTE

1.   Chris Harrison, "What Is a Sling?" Slinging.org, accessed July 09, 2016, http://slinging.org; Ludwik Siedlecki, "David's Sling: A Piece of History," Slinging.org, accessed July 09, 2016, http://slinging.org/index.php?page=david-s-sling-a-piece-of-history---ludwik-siedlecki; Gary Byers, "David's Sling and Stones: Were They Toys or Serious Weapons?" Christiananswers.net, accessed July 09, 2016, http://www.christiananswers.net/q-abr/abr-slingsforkids.html.

QUESTIONS TO PONDER

1. What are the weapons that you need to overcome the giants in your life?

_____

_____

_____

_____

_____

_____

_____

_____

2. What weapons do you already have?

_____

_____

_____

_____

_____

_____

_____

_____

_____

3. What is your vision? Is it founded on God's abundance, and does it line up with God's word? Reflect on the following questions prayerfully:

    - Have you released it to grow, and has it come to pass?

- Do you keep your vision under a cloud of doubt based on thoughts of lack, fear of the unknown, or your own personal limitations?

_____

_____

_____

_____

_____

_____

DECLARATION

I am armed with the mighty and surprising spiritual weapons of God. As I become more and more like my Father, I act as God's secret weapon and surprise attack against the enemy. Like David, I will win against my giants as I listen to God's direction and choose the right weapon for every battle.

RULE 11

SPEAK UP

David said to the Philistine, "You come against me with sword and spear and javelin, but I come against you in the name of the Lord Almighty, the God of the armies of Israel, whom you have defied. This day the Lord will deliver you into my hands, and I'll strike you down and cut off your head. This very day I will give the carcasses of the Philistine army to the birds and the wild animals, and the whole world will know that there is a God in Israel. All those gathered here will know that it is not by sword or spear that the Lord saves; for the battle is the Lord's, and he will give all of you into our hands."

—1 SAMUEL 17:45–47

David spoke to the giant and declared his intentions. He didn't run around the camp looking for input on how to deal with the situation. He spoke with a few people to get information about the situation, he appeared before the king to get permission to fight the giant, and then he attacked. Just prior to attacking, he spoke to the giant, telling him that he would soon be defeated. We could learn a lot from David's example. Many of us spend too much time talking about our giants and not enough time talking to our giants. We call our friends, talk about it at church, and complain to our neighbors. We run through all our relationships, looking for a sympathetic ear. We talk to everyone else, when what we should be doing is talking to our giant—just like David did.

When David faced Goliath and declared his victory, he tapped into a spiritual truth that is absolutely essential to our victory over the giants of this life. David understood the power of our words. He understood that what we say matters because it actually creates our reality. It is as Joseph Garlington says: "Nothing happens in the Kingdom until something is said."[1] Before the battle began, David and Goliath exchanged words. Both men declared their victory. Both men made threats. Goliath made his statements in pride. He believed himself invincible and his opponent unworthy. But David made his statements in faith. He knew the God of the impossible was on his side, and therefore it was the giant who was unworthy. By declaring this, David partnered with the unseen realm of Heaven and brought Heaven's reality into manifestation on earth. In David's three statements to Goliath, he shows us three keys to speaking up powerfully against the giants in our world.

First, David said, "In the name of the Lord." David publicly declared his allegiance to God. He was not fighting in his own name, but in the name of the one who had sent him. Like him, we are here on God's business. We are fighting in the name of the Lord. This truth comes with great responsibility, but it also comes with great authority. David recognized this authority, and he knew it meant his victory over the giant was assured.

Second, David said, "The Lord will deliver you into my hand." David spoke his own future, and he saw victory before it ever happened. David knew the battle belonged to the Lord, and it was He who would give the victory. It is one thing to whisper "God has the victory" to ourselves in private. It is quite another to stand eye to eye with our giant and say it to his face. Part of invoking the authority of Heaven is having the confidence to declare the truths of God's Kingdom in the face of the enemy.

David could confidently declare his victory because he knew God personally. He had an intimate understanding of God's desire to provide the victory on that battlefield, and this led him to speak with bold faith. We are not meant to make declarations from a place of doubt or even a place of blind faith. Sometimes we need to make these kinds of declarations without the personal, experiential knowledge of their truth. But, I believe David had seen the character of God when he spent time with Him in the fields with the sheep. He knew God, and that relationship gave him the confidence to speak this truth.

Third, David said, "That all the earth may know that there is a God in Israel." David saw this challenge as something bigger than just a battle between himself and a giant. He faced it with a higher purpose. David ran to the battle so that the world would know that God would give him victory. Knowing that every victory is not only a victory for us but also a victory for the Kingdom brings a healthy weight to all our battles.

In each of these three statements, we see that David's focus was on the bigger picture. To him, Goliath was not just a giant. He was a spiritual assignment, and David positioned his words accordingly. This is something many Christians fail to do. We get stuck in our own little worlds, and we do not see the big picture impact of the battles we face. We see them from an earthly perspective instead of a heavenly one. As a result, we often forget to use the power of our words to align with Heaven's plan for our battle, and too often we are easily overcome. To be giant slayers, we must learn to first see our situations from Heaven's perspective and, second, use our words to bring Heaven's reality to earth.

The Bible is full of heroes who recognized the higher purpose their actions represented. Noah could overcome the scoffing of people because he had a purpose. Abraham could leave his home for a new land because he had a purpose. Joseph had strength to endure a dark prison because he had a dream. Daniel could sleep in a lions' den because he believed in a higher purpose. Shadrach, Meshach, and Abednego could enter a fiery furnace because they had a purpose. John the Baptist could live life in the wilderness because he had a purpose. Stephen preached and died for an unpopular gospel because of purpose. Paul endured torture, slander, and shipwreck because he had a purpose. Jesus, our example, endured the cross because of His higher purpose.

We all have a higher purpose. God has set each of us up for greatness in His Kingdom. No one is a pawn in His game of chess. We are all key elements in His plan to bring Heaven to earth. To partner with His plan, we need to learn to speak up. Much of our warfare involves wielding the power of our words.

The Power of Our Words

Our words are more powerful than many of us know. The Bible tells us this over and over. More than eighty Scriptures address the power of the tongue. This is because we are made in the image of God, and God uses His words to create. In fact, the very first thing we see God doing in the Bible is speaking the world into existence (see Gen. 1:1–3). God created the world and every living thing in it with His words. When He spoke in Genesis 1, nothing became something. The word for *created* in Genesis 1:1 literally means "something from nothing." God said it, and it was so. It is hard for us to wrap our minds around this reality, but this is the power of God's voice. When God speaks, He creates. The author of Hebrews describes it like this: *"By faith we understand that the universe was formed at God's command, so that what is seen was not made out of what was visible"* (Heb. 11:3). God created the tangible universe using nothing but the power of His words.

Not only that, but when He created humanity He made us in His image. He made us to be creators in imitation of Him as the Creator. We are made to create realities just like He does. This is why our words carry so much power. The words we speak over our circumstances, the people around us, and ourselves carry tremendous weight. Each word that comes from our mouths has the opportunity to create life or to create death. Proverbs 18:21 tells us, *"The tongue has the power of life and death, and those who love it will eat its fruit."* This is not just a metaphor for how our words affect the hearts of others. Yes, that is true. We can choose to either heal or hurt with our words. But, this is more than an emotional reality. Our words carry spiritual impact and can literally impart life or death to people and situations. This is why what we say matters so much. We can choose to speak victory over ourselves or victory over our giants.

We see this in the example of Jesus. One of the names the Bible uses for Jesus is *the Word:*

> *In the beginning was the Word, and the Word was with God, and the Word was God. He was with God in the beginning. Through him all things were made; without him nothing was made that has been made.*
>
> —JOHN 1:1-3

As *the Word,* Jesus often used His words to release the power of God and create Heaven's realities on earth. When He spoke, things happened. For example, when He spoke to diseases, they were healed (see Luke 4:40). When He spoke to demons, they had to leave (see Luke 4:41). And even when He spoke to death, it had to release its hold on people (see John 11:43). Jesus repeatedly demonstrated the power of the spoken word, and He challenged His followers to do the same. He told them:

> *Truly I tell you, if anyone says to this mountain, "Go, throw yourself into the sea," and does not doubt in their heart but believes that what they say will happen, it will be done for*

them. Therefore I tell you, whatever you ask for in prayer, believe that you have received it, and it will be yours.

—MARK 11:23-24

When we are filled with the Holy Spirit, His words on our lips are charged with heavenly authority. As a result, physical realities can be created and changed through our words. When we see a giant towering before us like a mountain, threatening God's plan for our lives, we have the authority, in faith, to tell that giant to drown itself in the ocean. Like Joshua and the people of Israel, we have the authority to shout down the walls that try to keep us from the promises of God (see Josh. 6:16). When the nation shouted in unison, the walls that stood between them and their destiny crumbled. Like Jesus, when we encounter a storm that threatens to sink our boat, we can speak to that storm and the wind and waves will be still (see Matt. 8:25-26). Instead of talking about how bad the storm is (like the disciples did), we can simply follow Jesus' example and speak out our authority over it.

Jesus has sent us into the world with a message. This message involves what we do, but it begins with what we say. When Jesus sent His disciples on their first missionary journey, He gave them a two-part mission: *"He sent them out to proclaim the kingdom of God and to heal the sick"* (Luke 9:2). He also told His disciples to go from place to place and speak "Peace!" to that place (see Luke 10:5). They should declare the Kingdom of God and then perform miracles to confirm that Kingdom. Our commission has not changed. With our words, we create atmospheres where people can receive the good news of Jesus' love, and with our words we release miracles that demonstrate the goodness of God.

The destinies of nations and cities and individuals are shaped by our declarations. If the spoken word can move a mountain, then it can remove cancer, solve marriage problems, restore rebellious children, and even bring revival to a dead church. Action is always needed to bring change, but most actions begin their life as words. If we want to defeat the giants we face, we need to speak up. We need to join with the anthems of Heaven and declare God's Kingdom purposes wherever we go. When we do, His Kingdom truly will come, and His will truly will be done on earth as it is in Heaven (see Matt. 6:10).

PROTECTING OUR WORDS

Of course, believing in the power of our words is one thing. Actually changing the way we speak is another. Many of us have long-standing speech patterns that do not match our theology. Shad Helmstetter notes that behavioral research shows that as much as 77 percent of everything we think is negative or counterproductive.[2] He also notes that children, on average, hear the word *no* 148,000 times before they reach the age of eighteen.[3] It is easy to see how, even in otherwise healthy households, human beings can learn to think negatively about themselves and their circumstances.

All too often, these negative thoughts become negative words, and we begin to expect and empower defeat in our lives. Though we claim to believe in God's purposes, because of the way we speak we unknowingly empower the enemy. This is why it is important to think about the kind of words that come out of our mouths. The Book of Proverbs describes what happens when we speak negatively about ourselves and our lives: *"From the fruit of their mouth a person's stomach is filled; with the harvest of their lips they are satisfied"* (Prov. 18:20), and, *"You have been trapped by what you said, ensnared by the words of your mouth"* (Prov. 6:2).

This is a serious reality. If we say things like, "I have such bad luck," "That's killing me," "I can't ever get that right," or any other number of negative statements about our lives, we are assigning ourselves to failure. God has so much more in store for us, but to access it we need to believe that what He says about Himself and about us is true. We need to speak like we believe it. The question is: Are we contributing to our victory or to our defeat with the words we are speaking?

A few years ago, God took me on a twenty-eight-day journey of learning to protect my words and speak in alignment with His will. In June 2014, after years of severe pain from my previous back injury and car accident, I needed to have back surgery. During that season, I was facing a lot of giants. I felt surrounded, and it would have been easy for me to feel overwhelmed. Yet, just six days after surgery, as I lay in bed I felt the Holy Spirit tell me He wanted to teach me how to speak to my giants, not about them. It all began with perceiving life from His perspective and speaking from that revelation. He said to me, "I want you to see what I see, and I want you to think the way I think, and I want you to feel what I feel so that you can do what I do. But before you can do that, I want you to see *you* the way I see you, think about *you* the way I think about you, and love *you* the way I love you. Then you can do what I am doing in this situation."

So, for the next twenty-eight days, I looked in the mirror and started to see what He sees and come into agreement with it. I started to speak it out loud, by faith, even when it was the opposite of what I felt or perceived in the natural. The Holy Spirit had said He wanted me to see myself and think about myself and love myself the way He does—from a heavenly perspective. So I began asking Him, "How do You see me? What thoughts do You have about me? How much do You love me?" And as soon as I started to feel what His thoughts were toward me, I would speak them out loud and come into agreement with them. As I did this day after day, I started to see what He sees and think what He thinks and love what He loves about me. Each one of those things I spoke out loud by faith. In this way, I battled with my words to plant seeds for the future that would become a harvest based on what I was speaking. I knew I would reap the fruit of the words I was sowing, so I was careful to speak only what He sees and thinks, to speak about how great His love is for me.

By doing this, I shifted the environment both within me and around me. As I spoke God's words over my life and situation, my faith followed, and His victory seemed as certain to me as it was to David when he faced Goliath. If we want our words to have positive power, they must come from God, go through Him, and come back to Him. First, we receive His word. Second, we become His word. Third, we release His word. When we encounter giants, we speak the opposite according to the nature of God. This applies to any giant we may face. We can simply identify the opposite of the giant, God's truth that counters the giant's lie, and we declare it out loud. Doing this will cause transformation in our lives and will shift atmospheres.

For example, when I encountered the giant of fear, I spoke regarding my protection in Christ. I called myself bold and fearless, and I declared that God has not given me fear but power, love, and a sound mind. I would say, "I have the love, power, and wisdom in every moment that is needed to conquer fear." In this way, I mastered the way I was thinking, and I started to speak abundant life over myself. I was not overcome by my circumstances, but I chose to overcome them by agreeing with God's truth about them.

No matter what we experience, we must not let the circumstances of life determine what we say and do. Instead, we need to start talking about our lives the way God does. We have to treat our words as powerful, knowing that each thing that leaves our mouths carries great weight. We have to protect the words that come out of our mouths. If we don't, we will be doomed to live the lives we can make for ourselves instead of the lives He has built for us. Of course, it can be hard to put this into practice when we are face to face with a giant. This is why we must practice speaking the truth over ourselves *before* we are in a crisis moment. Then, our minds will be trained, like David's was, to declare the truth to our giants.

SPEAKING LIKE A GIANT SLAYER

To experience victory like David did, we must master our tongues like David did. We must speak like a giant slayer. Following are several practical ways we can avoid negative speech and cultivate positive speech in a way that will empower us to overcome the giants we face.

1. The Name of Jesus

The early church recognized the power of Jesus' name, and they regularly made declarations using His name to defeat giants. New believers received the forgiveness of their sins by praying and being baptized in the name of Jesus (see 1 Cor. 6:11; Acts 10:48; 19:5). When Peter encountered the lame man outside the Temple, he recognized that Jesus' name had the power to heal that man. So he said, *"In the name of Jesus Christ of Nazareth, walk"* (Acts 3:6). Immediately, the man was healed. And Paul, when he wanted to free a demon-possessed girl from bondage, commanded the spirit to leave her in Jesus' name (see Acts 16:18).

In fact, the early believers performed such incredible feats using the name of Jesus that even among unbelievers *"the name of the Lord Jesus was held in high honor"* (Acts 19:17). The name of Jesus is stronger than any giant. For this reason, our lives should be filled with declarations of His name and purpose. As Paul said, *"And whatever you do, whether in word or deed, do it all in the name of the Lord Jesus, giving thanks to God the Father through him"* (Col. 3:17). His name is always the most powerful thing we can say.

2. Recitation of Scripture

The Bible is God's revealed truth. When we are in the midst of difficulty, it is an objective voice that can remind us of what God says about our situation. One of the best ways to combat the negative thoughts of the enemy is to read Scripture out loud and make it personal to our lives. This is how we renew our minds, as the apostle Paul says in Romans 12:2:

> *Do not conform to the pattern of this world, but be transformed by the renewing of your mind. Then you will be able to test and approve what God's will is—his good, pleasing and perfect will.*

The pattern of this world is negativity. But when we renew our minds with Scripture, we can know and declare God's good, pleasing, and perfect will over our lives.

3. Declarations of Identity

Much of the enemy's strategy against us involves lying to us about who we are. For this reason, declaring out loud our new creation identity in Christ is a powerful weapon against the enemy. We are the children of God, royal heirs to His Kingdom, and when we declare that, giants must bow. Once, I saw this happen in a powerful way in Tanzania. During a meeting, I led the people in calling out to God as their Father—*Baba* in Swahili. As the people spoke aloud the truth that God is their Father, we experienced a great outpouring of healing and deliverance. One of the greatest declarations we can make against the enemy and his forces is this—God is our Father, and we are His beloved children. The reality of Heaven comes down to earth when we call Him Father. By doing so, we are declaring our position in Christ, seated in the heavenlies, and we are declaring our authority over the forces of darkness (see Eph. 2:6). It is no wonder that when Jesus taught His disciples to pray He started with, *"Our Father"* (Matt. 6:9).

4. Prophecies of Destiny

Not only can we declare our identity, but we can also declare the prophetic words over our lives. This is exactly what Ezekiel did in the vision of the dry bones. God told Ezekiel He had a plan for those bones. They hadn't fulfilled their destiny yet. So, based on God's plan, Ezekiel spoke to those bones: *"This is what the Sovereign Lord says to these bones: I will make breath enter you, and you will come to life"* (Ezek. 37:5). And it happened exactly as Ezekiel had prophesied. In the same way, when we know God's destiny for our lives, we can use our words to agree with God's plan. The enemy wants us to doubt what God said or to ask, *How can that possibly happen now? Perhaps God has given up on me.* Words like these introduce doubt into our destiny and can prevent us from the fullness that God has planned for us. Instead, we must declare what God has said, even when it seems as impossible as dry bones coming back to life.

These four tools will help us train our speech to align with Heaven, to speak up like the giant slayers we are, and to refuse to allow the lies of the enemy to come between us and our destiny. If we are going to be giant slayers, then we need to start speaking like giant slayers. We can't afford to talk about the giants' enormity and power without also talking about God's grace to overcome them. We must remain focused, staring our giants in the eyes and declaring the will of God. It is time for us to start sending out our words like weapons. It is time to start paving the road to victory with our declarations. Every declaration breeds an action. The question is, what are we declaring? When we spread good words like seeds throughout our lives and the lives of others, we cannot help but reap a great harvest soon.

NOTE

1.   Quoted in Bill Johnson, *Dreaming with God* (Shippensburg, PA: Destiny Image, 2006), 174.
2.   Shad Helmstetter, *What to Say When You Talk to Yourself* (New York, NY: Pocket Books, 1982), 21.
3.   Shad Helmstetter, *Choices: Discover Your 100 Most Important Life Choices* (New York, NY: Pocket Books, 1990).

QUESTIONS TO PONDER

1. Do you hurt yourself with your words? What negative things have you spoken over yourself? List them and then repent for not thinking of yourself the way God does.

_____

_____

_____

_____

_____

_____

2. Read Philippians 4:8. List all of the positive thoughts God has for you.

_____

_____

_____

_____

_____

3. Identify the things in the Philippians 4:8 list that dominate your thinking, those that only cross your mind occasionally, and those that never seem to find their way into your mind. Which of God's thoughts do you find hard to believe in a real and tangible way?

_____

_____

_____

_____

_____

_____

4. When facing Goliath, David made declarations of faith. Reflect on this statement: _Don't use your words to describe your situation; use your words to change your situation._ Do you feel your faith declarations are fearful (timid) or bold? Explain:

_____

_____

_____

_____

_____

_____

_____

_____

5. Words are a clear indicator of what is hiding in the heart. Check what is coming out of your mouth. Ask your close friends and loved ones what they hear you saying about yourself. Have you been talking like an overcomer?

_____

_____

_____

_____

_____

_____

_____

_____

DECLARATION

I am a child of God. He is my Father, and He has made me in His image. He has made me to be a giant slayer and an overcomer. He has put His creative power in my words, and from this day forward I will use my words in alignment with Heaven. I will agree with His truth and disagree with the doubts, fears, and lies of the enemy.

RULE 12

RUN FORWARD

As the Philistine moved closer to attack him, David ran quickly toward the battle line to meet him.

—1 SAMUEL 17:48

One of the most stunning visuals of the story of David and Goliath is the moment when the young David, who is wearing no armor and carrying no sword, begins to run quickly toward the well-armed Goliath. He does not walk forward or wait for the giant to come to him. No, he rushes full-force ahead. I imagine everyone watching held their breath, amazed by his courage and wondering what would happen. In this final stage of David's confrontation with Goliath, we find two important keys to his victory: He ran forward, and he fought until the battle was done.

This he did in a way that foreshadows the king he would become. Though he had been anointed as the future king in First Samuel 16, this was his first kingly act. The traditions of the time dictated that the king should lead his soldiers into battle, but Saul, the present king, was hiding in his tent. So David, who had the heart of a king, took the initiative and confronted the giant. Saul's response to Goliath's threat was to run away and hide. David's response was to run forward and fight.

In these two men we see the two options we have when a giant stands in our way. We can run forward to fight, or we can flee in search of safety. The choice between these two responses is often referred to as "fight or flight." Our bodies have chemical systems that activate during moments of perceived danger and release adrenaline and cortisol. These hormones speed the heart rate, slow digestion, increase blood flow to large muscle groups, and dilate the eyes. This gives our bodies a burst of energy and strength, preparing us to either run for our lives or fight for our lives.

Most animals have similar systems. Over the years, prey animals (such as deer, rabbits, and antelope) have developed a stronger sense of "flight" when the fight-or-flight response is triggered because these kinds of animals are often hunted by predators. These animals have learned that it's best to run when they feel fear. People sometimes develop the same instinct, especially when they experience trauma at an age when they are incapable of protecting themselves.

While the fight-or-flight response is an important and God-given mechanism to keep us from harm, sometimes life's lessons can teach us wrongly. At times, running from a situation is the wise choice. For example, God told Mary and Joseph to flee Herod's wrath, and it was certainly wise for Joseph to run from Potiphar's wife when she tried to seduce him (see Matt. 2:13; Gen. 39:6-12). In these instances, they did not run away because of fear; they ran away because of wisdom. However, many times this is not the case. Many times when we run away, it is not because it is the wisest choice but because we are afraid to face our problems. The more we do this, the more natural and right it feels. If we become too accustomed to running from our problems, it can be hard for us to turn and fight when the time is right.

Obviously, if we want to become giant slayers who transform the world like David, then we need to learn to be the ones who run toward our problems instead of away from them. We need to be less like Saul, who hid in his tent, and we need to be more like David, who ran bravely forward. Saul's son, Jonathan, gives us another example of what it looks like to run forward in battle. In an earlier skirmish with the Philistines, while King Saul and the Israelite army hid, Jonathan said to his armor bearer:

> Come, let's go over to the outpost of those uncircumcised men. Perhaps the Lord will act in our behalf. Nothing can hinder the Lord from saving, whether by many or by few.
>
> —1 SAMUEL 14:6

So, they snuck off to confront the enemy, just the two of them. To reach the Philistine outpost, they had to climb, using their hands and feet, up a narrow pass with sheer cliffs on either side. This was no easy venture. Because they had to climb up to the enemy, they had a significant disadvantage, yet Jonathan led the way with his armor bearer behind him, and together they killed about twenty men. This caused mass confusion and fear in the Philistine camp, and as a result, the Israelites were able to defeat the Philistine army.

Jonathan and his armor bearer ran courageously toward their giant of impossibility by climbing up to meet the enemy. Instead of hiding in fear from a problem that seemed too big for them, they ran forward in faith, and as a result they won a great victory. It is no wonder that Jonathan later gave his allegiance to David instead of his own father. He shared the same warrior spirit. Like Jonathan and David, if we are to become giant slayers, we must learn when it is time to stop running away and to start running forward.

No More Running Away

Ten years ago, I discovered the danger of running away from the giants of life. One of the biggest personal giants I have faced is the giant of pain from the injuries I experienced to my neck and back, first in the swimming pool and then in the car accident. I never fully recovered from these injuries. Instead, I was experiencing more and more pain and, as a result, using stronger pain medications just to get by. Eventually, in 2003, I began abusing the medication. This lasted for two years, until I checked myself into a treatment facility in 2005. As I described in chapter 5, this was the darkest season of my life, not only because I felt lost, alone, and ashamed, but also because I could not feel God's presence. For five months, though I cried out to God, I heard nothing from Him. At the end of this season, God's presence did return, and slowly I began to recover.

After I had fully recovered from my addiction, I finally came to understand why I had become so completely trapped in the vicious cycle of pain and addiction. I realized I had believed I had to earn my place in God's heart by serving Him well. I didn't realize that He meant for me to serve him well because I was already in His heart and on His mind. Instead of running forward into battle against this giant of pain and addiction, I had run and run in the opposite direction, terrified of having to face my problems. While I ran, my giant grew bigger and stronger until it was too big for me to run from.

Because I chose to run away, in the end I had to fight a much larger giant to regain my freedom. Not only did I need to fight the giant of pain and addiction, but I also needed to fight the lies I had believed about God's heart toward me. This fight was the darkest season of my life—in part because I had allowed the enemy to chase me into a corner. I had so much ground to recover, especially in my heart and mind. One of the lessons I learned from that season is the value of facing our giants at the right time—the value of running forward instead of running away.

We all have a choice between fight and flight. We each must choose whether we will run toward our giants or away from them. No one else can do it for us. We are each equally personally responsible, regardless of our position in life, to face our own giants. The choice is ours alone. We can run toward our giants and fight them, or we can run away, giving our giants time to grow larger and stronger. It is crucial, if we want to live in victory, that we stop running away. It is time to turn, to face those giants, and to bravely run forward.

COURAGE FOR THE PROBLEM

Running forward toward the enemy, of course, takes a great deal of courage. If showing up to the battle is the first step of courage, running toward our giant is the second. We've already talked about the need to face our fears. One reason why many of us lack the courage we need to run forward is our lack of perspective. We see the presence of problems in our lives as a negative. We allow them to discourage us and get in the way of our victories. That is exactly what the enemy intends. He wants to distract us from our destiny through these giants. Often, they are the reason why people don't reach the fulfillment of their lifelong passions.

This fear of our problems is a bigger problem than the problem, as Steve Backlund often says. Instead of allowing giants to intimidate us, we need to see our problems the way God does—as stepping stones toward our destiny. When we face and defeat the giants we are called to fight, doing so will propel us forward. If David had not faced Goliath, he would have remained an unknown shepherd boy. Likewise, when we face our giants, God uses our victory over them to push us forward into our calling. Because of this, giants are actually a pivotal part of our ability to succeed. Yet many of us, not realizing the benefit of overcoming giants, try to avoid the problems along our path. We become very good at running away.

When we do so, we are only sabotaging our own destiny. Instead, we must learn to approach the problem of these giants in the right way. We must learn to understand the nature of problems. Too many times, I have seen people who burned with passion and were ready to conquer the world lose their fire because they weren't ready to face the obstacles on the road to their victory. To help us avoid the same end, here I have listed five truths about the nature of problems. Understanding these truths will give us perspective so that we will be courageous enough to run forward into battle.

1. All God's children have problems.

It's easy to look at someone else's life and wish we had what they have. If I had as much money as he does, all my problems would be solved. I wouldn't be so insecure if I was as talented as she is. I would be fine if I had his job. Everything would be perfect if I was as lucky as she is. The truth is, everyone has problems, and no amount of talent, money, education, or support will help us avoid them. Other people may not have the same problems that we do, but they have their own set of equally overwhelming issues. Accepting this reality helps us avoid wasting our time in the trap of envy, and it helps us focus on creating solutions to the problems we face. Problems are a part of the process of victory. Accepting this will bring purpose to every battle.

2. Without problems, we cannot have success.

A wise philosopher once commented that an eagle's only obstacle to flying with greater speed and ease is the air. Yet, if the air was withdrawn, the proud bird would be attempting to fly in a vacuum and instantly fall to the ground, unable to fly at all. Resistance is the catalyst of success. The only reason a thing has not been done is that no one has yet discovered a way to overcome the problems that keep us from it. Every invention is the result of someone overcoming a problem. Every history book is filled with great men and women who overcame great problems. To eliminate the existence of problems is to eliminate the possibility of greatness. Recognizing this helps us to stop trying to avoid our problems and to start pursuing ways to overcome them.

In the life of David, God used the victory over Goliath to position David for his ascension to the throne and to prepare David for future victories. Facing the giant was a doorway to a new level of anointing.

3. Problems are our friends, not our enemies.

A proper perspective will turn our problems into our friends. If we recognize that problems are part of the process of victory, then we will keep these problems close in our minds. We will embrace them as a challenge and an invitation to greatness, not as a hopeless struggle. When we keep our problems in mind, we make room for the Holy Spirit to speak His solution to us. The fact is, God already knows the solution for every problem we face, and as His children we have access to His solutions. We simply need to adjust our perspective and listen for His voice.

All great leaders have to overcome tremendous problems in their lives. We are not the exceptions to the rule. In his book *Developing the Leader Within You,* John Maxwell writes that a study of three hundred highly successful people (such as Helen Keller, Winston Churchill, Albert Schweitzer, Mahatma Gandhi, and Albert Einstein) reveals that one in four had physical handicaps, such as blindness, deafness, or crippled limbs. Three in four had either been born in poverty, came from a broken home, or at least came from exceedingly painful or disturbed situations.[1]

In other words, our problems are not an excuse for failure. Instead, we are meant to be overcomers and giant slayers, which means problems and giants will be in our path. This should not discourage us. Instead, it should encourage us that we are created to defeat the giants in our lives. It is part of who we are made to be. Thus, instead of running from problems,

GIANT SLAYERS

we should embrace them as doors to our destiny. Being well acquainted with our problems equips us to run forward and overcome them.

4. The size of the leader is more important than the size of the problem.

There are no big problems or small problems, only big people and small people. What this means is that if our problems are too big for us, God is about to make us bigger. He is about to expand us so we have the capacity to overcome our problems. When David faced the big problem of Goliath, he asked questions, analyzed the problem, and took action. Recognizing that the situation was about to become a national crisis, David faced the issue head-on. He solved the problem of Goliath—not because he was the strongest, the meanest, or the bravest, but because he knew he was at the place of his assignment, and he believed God would give him the wisdom to solve the problem. Knowing who he was in God enabled David to become a big enough person to defeat the giant. Instead of running away and allowing the crisis to escalate, David ran forward, believing that God would help him win.

At times, we will run into problems that are too big for us. This is not because God has put us into impossible situations but because He has destined us to become bigger than we are. Through the wisdom and power of the Holy Spirit, we will grow and mature to become the kind of people who can overcome any obstacle. This is our destiny. Often, the way God expands us is through giving us bigger giants to fight.

5. Problems do not need to catch us off guard.

Great leaders are seldom caught off guard. They have developed the ability to sense a problem and to run forward and attack before the problem becomes a crisis. David slew Goliath, stopping the attack of the Philistines and preventing a much longer and bloodier war. The more experience we gain in fighting giants, the easier it will be for us to see them coming. Every battle we fight prepares us to fight future battles with

210

greater skill and confidence. Our victories propel us into greater victories. Having the boldness and assertiveness to attack our problems before they become a crisis prevents us from being overwhelmed by our problems.

These five truths give us the perspective we need to see that our problems are just speed bumps on the road to our greatest victories. Giants will come, but if we see them as stepping stones to destiny, we will have the courage to run toward them and the wisdom to win.

FINISHING THE JOB

When we commit to running forward toward our giants, we commit to finishing the job. This is exactly what David did. When he began running forward, he knew that doing so meant there would be no other way out. It would be too late for him to turn around and run away. He was committed to the end. He would win, or he would die. David not only ran to meet Goliath in battle, but he fought until the fight was over. He fought until Goliath had lost his head and the Philistines had been plundered (see 1 Sam. 17:50–54). This is important, because when God wants something done He wants it done all the way. If we leave a semi-defeated giant in our lives, that giant will come back to hurt us.

God warned the children of Israel about this when they entered the Promised Land. They had run forward into battle and defeated the giants in the land. Now, they needed to finish the job by purging the land. He told them to completely destroy all the idols they found there, and He forbade them from making treaties with the idol-worshiping people who lived there. He said this because He did not want them to come back later, put the idols back together, and worship them. He also did not want them to be obligated to pay homage to idols because of political treaties. God gave a solemn command and a clear picture of His attitude toward idols:

> *Be careful not to make a treaty with those who live in the land where you are going, or they will be a snare among you. Break*

*down their altars, smash their sacred stones and cut down their
Asherah poles.*

—EXODUS 34:12-13

He did not want the people to carefully take the idols apart piece by piece, but to break, smash, and cut them down so they could never be rebuilt. If they failed to do this, these idols and the people who served them would become a snare to the Israelites. Though God could have simply destroyed the idols Himself, He asked the people to do it instead. He knew that if they did not loathe the idols from their hearts, they would turn to them in years to come. Sadly, that is exactly what they did.

The same principle is true in our lives. It is not enough to fight our giants. We must persevere through until the fight is completed and the giant is fully defeated. We must fight until there is no chance of that giant rearing its head once again. Whether our giants are on the outside or the inside of our hearts, God wants us to take the weapons at our disposal and destroy them completely. He will be there to protect and guide us to victory, but He wants us to do it. He wants us to finish the job. God wants the victory to come by His power, but through our hands. He is a good Father, training us to be mature sons and daughters who are adept giant slayers.

FINISHING STRONG

In order to finish the job, we need to finish strong. We need to persevere to the end. This is not always easy. The passion that comes at the beginning of a fight can wane if the fight wears on. I believe David displayed three keys that helped make his fight with Goliath, as well as many of his future battles, strong to the end.

212

Preparation

First, David came to the battle prepared. The development of David's heart did not start on the day he met Goliath on the battlefield. It's foolish to believe we can fight giants without having prepared ahead of time. Instead, as the apostle Paul says, *"Everyone who competes in the games goes into strict training"* (1 Cor. 9:25). Just as athletes prepare for competition well in advance of the event, so we ought to prepare ourselves spiritually before we face giants. Otherwise, we won't be ready to fight the battle when we find ourselves on the front line. When the door of opportunity opens, it's too late to prepare.

David prepared first in the presence of God as he tended the sheep. This gave him the courage and confidence to know how to respond to the giant's threats, seek permission from the king, and run forward to face the giant in battle. He also took time to prepare his weapons, carefully selecting smooth stones to use for his sling.

Endurance

Second, David used endurance to keep fighting till the end. He modeled what it looks like to *"run with endurance the race that is set before us"* (Heb. 12:1 NKJV). The Greek word here for *endurance* is more literally translated "the patience to master." It is not a romantic ideal that gives us unending strength. It is unhurrying yet undelaying determination. Obstacles are a natural part of growth. Endurance understands the time needed to complete a task fully and is willing to engage it.

Runners call endurance the "second wind." It's when everything inside us is telling us to quit, but we tell our bodies not to. The ones who win are the ones who know how to push through the pain and never take their eyes off the finish line. Why would a runner get up before dawn, run hundreds of miles a week, endure hardship, bad weather, aching muscles and joints—and yet keep going? Runners do this because they know that at the end of the day, in order to win the prize, they must endure to the end. Those who don't have endurance—the patience to master—fail to see the purpose behind the pain, and they usually quit before the battle is complete.

Reproduction

Third, David knew his victory would reproduce in the lives of others. His victory was a victory for the armies of Israel, and it would shift the national perspective. His testimony would inspire courage in the hearts of the people. That is the nature of victory. It inspires those who are living in fear. When they see our victories, they will rise up in faith and also accomplish great things for God. Because they witness the defeat of a giant, they feel empowered to face their own giants, and they begin the process of becoming giant slayers.

People are watching how we handle our giants. If I am a coward, I will draw other cowards around me. If I am a giant slayer, I will draw other giant slayers around me. David became a giant slayer, and by doing so he inspired many others to be giant slayers. He reproduced who he was. We know the battle is truly won when our victory begins to multiply in the lives of others. David did this so well that later in his life, when he faced four more Philistine giants, he did not have to fight them alone.

David was now past the prime of his life, yet he was still going to battle with his men against the Philistines. Once again, the Philistines had produced giant warriors—the four sons of Goliath—to fight against the Israelites. The battle was fierce, and David grew tired. One of the giants, sensing David's weakness, pressed in and put David on the defensive. The enemy was about to kill the great giant slayer of Israel. But, because David had reproduced his victory in others, he was not left alone to die at the hand of the giant. Abishai came to his rescue and killed the giant on his behalf. Then, in successive battles, others of David's mighty men also killed the remaining three giants (see 2 Sam. 21:15–22).

This is the power of reproducing our victory and raising up other giant slayers. If David had not trained his mighty men, eventually he would have become too old to fight. By reproducing himself, he ensured that there would always be giant slayers in Israel. In the same way, if we are not passing down our victories to the next generation, then we are ensuring that our victories die with us. The best way to guarantee that the giants in the land are abolished forever is the raise up others to carry on the victory.

David ran forward, confidently and courageously, to confront Goliath, and he didn't stop fighting until the victory was completely won. Then, in the wake of his victory, he raised up many more giant slayers who could enforce the victory David had won even after David grew old. This is what it looks like to run bravely forward into battle and fight until the battle is completely won. We started this book talking about the importance of showing up to the battle. We can't win a battle we don't show up to. The other bookend to that truth is the need to run forward until the battle is done. To be giant slayers, we must not forget to fight the whole way through to completion.

This is the champion call. This is our destiny—not just mine but all of ours. While I don't know what other people's giants look like, I do know what it feels like to face a giant. I know what fear feels like. I know the grip of hopelessness and despair. Those moments in my life are all too easy for me to remember. But, I also remember the joy, peace, and absolute freedom that came when I finally decided to stop running and face my giants. I remember what it felt like to shed that burden that I had been carrying for so long and give it to God. And I know that if I can stand up and fight, then, by the grace of God, anyone can.

No matter what giants we face today, if we will simply turn and courageously face them, we can beat them. God has given us all we need. If we can't beat our giants alone, then He has put people around us to join the fight. If we don't have the energy or endurance, He is ready to teach us how to fight without growing weary. If we don't feel qualified, He is ready to present us with His qualifications. This is the bottom line: We are giant slayers, sons and daughters of God, born for victory and raised for glory. We must not let our giants lie to us, telling us we are anything less than that.

We will have many opportunities in our lives to choose to run forward toward the battle instead of running and hiding. In some seasons, we will have to do it every day. I have found myself in the middle of this tension dozens and dozens of times. Some of these times, as I've written about in this book, were in the midst of a deep personal crisis. Others were in the middle of great victory. Sometimes we run from big fears. Sometimes we run from small ones. Big or small, we must reach deep into our hearts and find the courage to turn, look our giants in the eye, and press the fight.

NOTE

1.   John Maxwell, *Developing the Leader Within You* (Nashville, TN: Thomas Nelson, 2005).

QUESTIONS TO PONDER

1. We discussed five statements about problems.

    * All God's children have problems.

    * Without problems, there can be no success.

    * Make problems your friends, not your enemies.

    * The size of the leader is more important than the size of the problem.

    * Problems do not need to catch us off guard.

    How can you apply the above statements to the problems you may be facing right now?

    _____

    _____

    _____

    _____

    _____

    _____

    _____

    _____

    _____

2. We discussed David's three keys to a strong finish. What steps will you take to ensure that you will finish strong? Explain:

    _____

    _____

    _____

    _____

    _____

3. In Second Timothy 4:6-7, the apostle Paul said, *"For I am already being poured out like a drink offering, and the time for my departure is near. I have fought the good fight, I have finished the race, I have kept the faith."* List some of the characteristics you think made Paul such a strong finisher:

    _____

    _____

    _____

    _____

    _____

    _____

    _____

4. Is it possible that you have been waiting for God to make a move, but God is waiting for you to stretch your faith? Is there something in your past that endangers your future? Take time and think through this question. It's possible it may be the most important question you answer!

    _____

    _____

    _____

    _____

    _____

    _____

    _____

DECLARATION

I declare that I will be a good steward of every gift and calling God has given me. I will not back away from any giant, real or perceived, that might block my destiny or my view of the greatness of God. Instead, I will run bravely forward into battle, confident that God is on my side and the victory is assured. I declare that I am born to be a giant slayer, and I always finish what I start. Like David, I will fight till the fight is completely won.

A WORLD OF GIANT SLAYERS

I have told you these things, so that in me you may have peace. In this world you will have trouble. But take heart! I have overcome the world.

—JOHN 16:33

We live in a world in need of giant slayers. We live in a world where corruption, pain, sorrow, fear, and doubt spread through the land like wildfire. We are divided by issues of race, gender, religion, and politics. It would be easy to look at the state of the world and see no hope. But that is not how God sees it. God sees a world full of His children. He sees His sons and daughters who are made in His image and made to thrive. He made each one of us to be more than conquerors, the light of the world, a city on a hill that cannot be hidden (see Rom. 8:37; Matt. 5:14–16). He made us to shine.

Our identity in Christ is a free gift. I can't imagine anything more precious, yet it is totally and completely free. We don't need to do anything to earn it. We only need to say *yes*. However, if we want to see the full measure of that identity expressed on the earth, we have to allow God to renew our hearts and minds and make us into mature sons and daughters. We have to learn to become giant slayers. To that end, in this book I have presented the twelve ground rules that will set us up to become mighty slayers of giants. No one of them is enough; they are all essential. Becoming a giant slayer is a lifetime process, and we cannot skip any part of the process.

David became a giant slayer as a boy, but he continued to slay giants and overcome obstacles for the rest of his days. If we want to live lives of victory after victory after victory, just like David, these ground rules will show us the way.

PULLING THE RULES TOGETHER

Here I will briefly summarize all the rules and illustrate how they work together to build us into the giant slayers we are destined to be. To help us apply these rules to our lives, we should meditate on them often and ask God for wisdom in knowing how to fully absorb them into our way of life. This is a process, but if we walk it out, we will begin to experience increasing measures of the blessing that God has given us. This is His desire for each one of us—that we would live in the fullness of our identity in Him and our destiny in this life.

Rule 1: Show Up

First, we must say *yes* to the call to become giant slayers. We have to decide to engage our giants. No one else can fight our battles for us. The victory is meant to belong to us. This is probably the most straightforward of all the ground rules, but in many ways it is the most essential. If we want victory, we have to show up to the battle. This may look like deciding to show up to work and give our best. This may look like showing up to propose an idea to one of our leaders. This may look like simply having the courage to get out of bed and face a new day. It probably looks different for each one of us, but I know that in our heart of hearts we will each know what we need to show up to. Let's do it now, today. We will be glad we did.

Rule 2: Find the Right Battle

Second, we must not waste our time and energy fighting a battle that doesn't belong to us. Not every fight is ours to fight. Or, maybe a fight is ours, but we have not yet prepared for it. Maybe we have to fight the fight to be diligent before we are ready to fight to make our dreams come true. Remember, we each have an assignment. We each have a place that God meant for us to be. He has put everything we need to know in our hearts. We simply need to take the time to discover all that He has planned for us.

Rule 3: Understand Timing

Third, we need a deeper understanding of God's ways and timing. He wants us to understand how He thinks and how He works. He wants us to know how to operate within His timeframe. Part of becoming a mature Christian is learning how to understand God's timing. We have to learn to become familiar with what season we are in. Otherwise, we will store things up when it's time to give them away or run and fight when it's time to prepare. Part of becoming a giant slayer is learning God's perception of time. He wants to build within us a new familiarity with His presence in the normal *Chronos* day-to-day goings-on of our lives. He also wants to build patience and diligence during our *Chronos* seasons that will prepare us to dive in head first when we arrive at our *Kairos* moments of opportunity.

Rule 4: Align with God and Others

Fourth, we must properly align ourselves in covenant with God and with other believers. David saw that the armies of Israel were terrified of an enemy that didn't even have a relationship with God. He knew that the covenant God had with His people would guarantee his success against Goliath. Knowing that God has made covenant promises with us is the only way to truly create the kind of courage needed to face the giants in our lives. We are also designed to be a people of covenant and connection with one another. We are meant to have brothers and sisters around us who give us strength when we are weak and remind us of the covenant we have with God.

Rule 5: Don't Lose Heart

Fifth, we must cultivate a tenacious heart. David had the heart of a giant slayer. Even when the king had lost any hope of winning, the shepherd boy with a sling still stood strong. As giant slayers, we can never afford to lose heart. We cannot let disappointment and fear get the best of our destiny. If one dream dies, then we need to start growing another one. The heart is the very center of what it means to be a giant slayer. Building our intimacy with God step by step will strengthen and expand our hearts until nothing can stop us. In the simplicity of our day-to-day lives, God is developing in us the hearts of giant slayers.

Rule 6: Ignore Critics and Face Fear

Sixth, we must learn to ignore destructive criticism and the fear it tries to invoke. No one ever did anything great without someone saying it was impossible. Fear tries to derail all of us. Those who have been shut down by fear oftentimes feel intimidated by those who are on their way to success. Criticism is the tool of the powerless. Those who give healthy corrective feedback always release it in a way that breeds life, while critics only release lifelessness. To be giant slayers, we must learn to face our fears and personal doubts even in the face of critics. All the greatest men and women in history experienced fear, especially when faced with impossible tasks. History remembers them because they chose not to let fear or criticism dissuade them.

Rule 7: Celebrate Past Victories

Seventh, we must learn to regularly celebrate past victories. What good are victories if we cannot remember them? Why would God give us something new if we have not celebrated what He has already given to us? We all have a history with God. Some of us have a longer history than others, but we all have one. We have to learn to gain strength from our past victories, to bring old testimonies into new situations. No matter how many giants we have defeated, we will always be in the same position. We will have victories behind us, we will be in the middle of fighting our current giant, and we will have giants that are still ahead. Some of us have more victories than others, but our place in life never really changes. If we can't learn to celebrate what God has already done right now, another victory will not solve the problem. This is the day that the Lord has made. Let us rejoice and be glad in it.

Rule 8: Seek the Reward

Eighth, we must be conscious of the rewards inherent in fighting giants. Giants are not arbitrary obstacles. They are gateways to glory. God wants us to live victoriously on all fronts of life. He wants us to be successful with our finances, prosperous in our families, and rich in His presence. God does not want us to waste our time fighting meaningless battles. Everything the enemy intends for our harm, God can turn for our good. In this way, giants actually give us access to greater favor, more finances, and greater maturity. When we win in battle, we cannot afford to let the fear of pride keep us from receiving the good gifts our heavenly Father wants to give us. Godly blessing comes with the opportunity to grow in the maturity we need to manage it well.

Rule 9: Be Yourself

Ninth, we must never underestimate the power of being ourselves. God made each one of us into exactly the kind of giant slayer He wants us to be. We still have to grow into more mature versions of ourselves, but we must always remain ourselves. No one can fight giants like we do. Some giants may only be able to be defeated by someone who is walking in his or her unique identity. It can be easy to look at others and think that they are better off or that we need what they have. The truth is, if we do need what they have then God will give it to us. God knows and loves us more than anyone else possibly can. He has crafted us by hand to be unique expressions of His glory. We must not waste any of our time trying to fit in anyone else's box. We are His creation, and that is qualification enough.

Rule 10: Bring the Right Weapons

Tenth, we must discern the proper weapon for every battle. Not all battles are won by brute force or in the conventional way. David defeated Goliath as a slinger, not as a soldier. Gideon defeated an army with clay pots and torches. God's ways are so much higher than ours. He is not the hero who comes riding in at the last second to save the day. He is the master craftsman who weaves our victory into the very fabric of our identity. A well-armed soldier could not defeat Goliath, but a slinging shepherd could. The same principle applies to our spiritual battles. God wants to teach us about the amazing arsenal of weapons that He has been training us with. These weapons within us may seem perfectly mundane and normal, but when we use them properly, we become weapons of immense power.

Rule 11: Speak Up

Eleventh, we must learn to use our voice to declare God's truth over every situation. We waste far too much time worrying about things that never happen. It's too easy to talk and talk about how big and overwhelming our problems are without buckling down and doing something about it. Words are the foundation of action. If we do not begin to temper our words to the presence of God, then we will sabotage our victories before they can even start. How we speak says a lot about what is going on inside our hearts. It reveals what God is working to remove so that we can be the victorious giant slayers He has designed us to be.

Rule 12: Run Forward

Twelfth, we must choose to run forward (not run away) and to fight till the finish. Instead of running away from our giants, we must cultivate the courage to run into battle, trusting that God is at our side. By doing this, we commit to the fight till the end. The fight with our giants is not over until it is over. There is no room for half measures in giant slaying. We must do it or not do it at all. Understanding the nature of problems and seeing them from Heaven's perspective will give us the courage we need to run forward. This is important because we will be facing giants for the rest of our lives. We do not want to spend our lives running away from giants and, as a result, allowing them to become bigger and stronger in our lives. Such giants, if we let them, will thwart our destiny and keep us from fulfilling our lifelong passions. God has destined us to release freedom on the earth. When we run forward in faith to defeat our giants, the victory we gain impacts the world for generations to come.

START TODAY

We do not have to wait to become giant slayers. David was just a boy when he faced Goliath. Actually, he started becoming a giant slayer long before that famous battle. David became a giant slayer in the fields with the sheep. He played his harp and became familiar with the presence of God. He developed a sensitivity to the Spirit of God that would serve and protect him for the rest of his days on the earth. It made him a great giant slayer and a great king. Like David, the main thing we need to do to become giant slayers is to cultivate intimacy with our heavenly Father's presence. He is with us at all times. His presence is resting on us, and His voice is speaking to our hearts, building our hearts into something strong.

We all have giants in our lives, and we can see the giants in the lives of others. What would it look like if they all started to fall, one by one? What if someone brought down the giant of racism once and for all? What if someone defeated the giant of atheism, or hunger, or lust? What would the world look like if those giants were simply gone? This is a vision of the world that should burn in our hearts. Defeating these giants is what we were made for—and so much more. After all, God doesn't need us to be giant slayers because there is too much evil in the world. No evil has ever intimidated Him. God wants us to be giant slayers so that we can make room for all the great and wondrous things He has planned to release on the earth. The good He has in store for all of us is so much greater than we can imagine (see Eph. 3:20). No mind can even begin to conceive of the magnitude of the glory that He is ready to release. All we have to do is prepare the way.

ABOUT LEIF HETLAND

Leif Hetland is founder and president of Global Mission Awareness. He ministers globally bringing an impartation of God's love, healing, and apostolic authority through a paradigm of Kingdom family. A forerunner in modern-day missions, Leif has brought the gospel into the most spiritually dark areas of the world. Over one million souls have been saved through his ministry.

He has written numerous books, including his best sellers *Seeing Through Heaven's Eyes* and *Healing the Orphan Spirit*.

OTHER RESOURCES FROM LEIF HETLAND

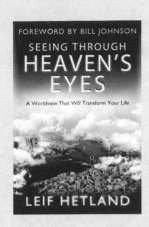

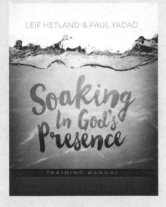

Available online at **shop.globalmissionawareness.com**

CONNECT WITH LEIF HETLAND

For information on events, ministry trips and the impact of Leif Hetland Ministries and Global Mission Awareness, visit:

www.globalmissionawareness.com

Facebook: facebook.com/leifhetland
Instagram: @leifhetland **Twitter:** @leifhetland